D1563228

"A Policy Calculated to Benefit China"

Recent Titles in
Contributions to the Study of World History

The Free Germany Movement: A Case of Patriotism or Treason?
Kai P. Schoenhals

Victims and Survivors: Displaced Persons and Other War Victims in Viet-Nam,
1954
Louis A. Wiesner

Tsar Paul and the Question of Madness: An Essay in History and Psychology
Hugh Ragsdale

The Orphan Stone: The Minnesinger Dream of Reich
Richard J. Berleth

American Constitutionalism Abroad: Selected Essays in Comparative Constitutional
History
George Athan Billias, editor

Appeasement in Europe: A Reassessment of U.S. Policies
David F. Schmitz and Richard D. Challener, editors

Ritual and Record: Sports Records and Quantification in Pre-Modern Societies
John Marshall Carter and Arnd Krüger, editors

Diverse Paths to Modernity in Southeastern Europe: Essays in National Development
Gerasimos Augustinos, editor

The Chinese Revolution in Historical Perspective
John E. Schrecker

Cities and Caliphs: On the Genesis of Arab Muslim Urbanism
Nezar AlSayyad

The French Revolution in Culture and Society
David G. Troyansky, Alfred Cismaru, and Norwood Andrews, Jr., editors

Russia and Italy Against Hitler: The Bolshevik-Fascist Rapprochement of the 1930s
J. Calvitt Clarke III

Germany and the Union of South Africa in the Nazi Period
Robert Citino

"A Policy Calculated to Benefit China"

The United States and the China Arms Embargo, 1919–1929

STEPHEN J. VALONE

Contributions to the Study of World History, Number 25

Greenwood Press
New York • Westport, Connecticut • London

Library of Congress Cataloging-in-Publication Data

Valone, Stephen J.
  "A policy calculated to benefit China" : the United States and the
China arms embargo, 1919-1929 / Stephen Valone.
    p. cm. — (Contributions to the study of world history, ISSN
0885-9159 ; no. 25)
  Includes bibliographical references and index.
  ISBN 0-313-27621-8 (alk. paper)
  1. United States—Foreign relations—China. 2. China—Foreign
relations—United States. 3. Military assistance, American—China—
History—20th century. 4. China—History—Warlord period,
1916-1928. I. Title. II. Series.
E183.8.C5V27   1991
327.73051—dc20   90-20734

British Library Cataloguing in Publication Data is available.

Library of Congress Catalog Card Number: 90-20734
ISBN: 0-313-27621-8
ISSN: 0885-9159

First published in 1991

Greenwood Press, 88 Post Road West, Westport, CT 06881
An imprint of Greenwood Publishing Group, Inc.

Printed in the United States of America

The paper used in this book complies with the
Permanent Paper Standard issued by the National
Information Standards Organization (Z39.48-1984).

10 9 8 7 6 5 4 3 2 1

Copyright Acknowledgment

The author and publisher gratefully acknowledge permission to reprint
material from the following copyrighted source.

Gavin McCormick. *Chang Tso-lin in Northeast China, 1911-1928: China,
Japan and the Manchurian Idea.* Stanford University Press, 1977.

[The State] Department has believed [the arms] embargo to be a policy calculated to benefit China as a whole if consistently applied over [a] considerable period and would not feel warranted in changing such [a] policy on account of the incidental strength of a faction whose leadership may not appear so commendable as the present government.

Secretary of State Charles Evans Hughes to
Minister Jacob Gould Schurman, 12 October 1922,
Department of State, National Archives

Contents

Reprinted with permission from *The Cambridge History of China*, volume 12, John K. Fairbank, editor, Cambridge University Press, 1986.

Preface

In the course of my work, I have acquired debts to many people that I wish to acknowledge. Professor MacGregor Knox of the University of Rochester provided friendly support and constructive criticism to me throughout this project. Professors Donald Bain and Mieczyslaw Biskupski hired me to teach at St. John Fisher College, which provided me with the financial resources to complete my work and get married. David MacGregor, Harry Hubbard, and the late Professor Robert B. Hall, Jr., each in his own way, provided friendship and encouragement when it was most needed. Over the years, my parents James and Geraldine Valone have helped me in more ways than they can realize. Most importantly, my wife Kim has always been there with love and patience as I have struggled to become a good scholar, teacher, and husband, all at the same time.

As John K. Fairbank noted on page xvii of the preface to volume 12 of *The Cambridge History of China*, the use of *pinyin* system for transcription of Chinese sounds into alphabetic writing would "greatly complicate the work of researchers." Accordingly, I have chosen to use the Wade-Giles romanization system in this book; for the sake of consistency, however, uniform spellings of Chinese names have been used throughout.

Introduction

China has fascinated many in the United States ever since the earliest days of the Republic. In 1784 the fifteen-month voyage from New York harbor to Canton of the merchantman *Empress of China* showed American businessmen that trade with China was both feasible and profitable. Thereafter the lure of the potentially lucrative "China market" steadily increased. At the same time the activity of a growing number of American missionaries served to foster interest in the Chinese people.

In spite of this expanding awareness of China, the United States did not dominate Chinese affairs. Great Britain formally established itself as the predominant power in China with the Opium War (1839-1842), which initiated the great powers' assault on Chinese sovereignty. Over the next two generations, mounting foreign encroachment stimulated popular dissatisfaction with the Peking government and seriously undermined the authority of the Manchu dynasty. In order to safeguard American trade and opportunity in China, Secretary of State John Hay issued the famous Open Door Notes in 1899 and 1900, which called upon the powers to cooperate with Washington in maintaining free access to China's wealth. With the Open Door Notes, Hay established a framework for U.S. Far Eastern policy for the next half century.

Since the formal inception of the Open Door in 1899, scholars have debated the origins and impact of the policy. Before World War I writers such as Alfred Thayer Mahan and Charles Conant viewed the Open Door policy favorably. They and others believed that it demonstrated that the United States had come of age as a great power, and was determined to defend its access to the world's markets.[1]

Many historians had second thoughts in the wake of World War I. Tyler Dennett, for example, who had considered the Open Door to have benefited all parties early in his career, questioned the value of the policy in the years before World War II. Indeed as the 1930s progressed, both Dennett and A. Whitney Griswold doubted whether the United States should defend the Open Door at the risk of war with Japan.[2]

World War II and the subsequent Cold War helped to rehabilitate the Open Door. Reminiscent of Mahan and Conant, writers such as Dexter Perkins and Walter Lippmann favored the onset of U.S. global responsibilities.[3] But by the 1950s many historians came to criticize the Open Door policy for leading the United States into overcommitting itself in areas not critical to national security.[4]

At the same time, however, a growing number of historians launched much more scathing attacks. These revisionists condemned the policy as an attempt to exploit China in order to expand the American economy. Such revisionist attacks on American foreign policy intensified during the 1960s.[5] As passions over the Vietnam conflict cooled, some historians countered the revisionist argument by contending that the Open Door policy had neither harmed China nor threatened Japan gravely enough to have caused conflict with the United States.[6]

Whatever the impact of Hay's notes on the foreign policy of the United States, within China the domestic unrest fueled by the Empire's manifest weaknesses continued to mount, until finally in October 1911 a revolution erupted that threatened to topple the Peking government. The next month, General Yüan Shih-k'ai was summoned back from a forced retirement of nearly three years and accepted the post of prime minister to suppress the revolt. Yüan undertook operations against the insurgents but soon realized that Manchu rule was beyond saving. He therefore proceeded to negotiate a truce with the rebels and then convinced the emperor to abdicate the throne on 12 February 1912. Within a matter of months, the revolutionaries accepted Yüan as the provisional president of the new Chinese Republic. Ultimately, Yüan betrayed the republican cause and by the fall of 1913 ruled China as a virtual dictator. Before his death in the summer of 1916, he even sought to install himself as emperor. In spite of his machinations, Yüan's four-year tenure as China's chief executive did at least provide a form of momentary political stability in Peking, for the revolution against the Manchus initiated nearly four decades of turmoil, which culminated in the triumph of Mao Tse-tung in 1949.

In the meantime, those powers with investments and/or aspirations in China, particularly Great Britain, Japan, Russia, and the United States, were confronted with ongoing civil unrest and war. The decade after Yüan's death was particularly perplexing in this regard. During that period, regional warlords vied constantly for control of Peking, and the capital was rife with rumors of their various intrigues.[7]

World War I further compounded China's difficulties, because Europe's weakened hold in Asia presented Tokyo with a unique opportunity to expand its influence.[8] The Japanese were quick to exploit this situation. After declaring war on Germany and occupying its possessions in China and the Pacific, Tokyo sought to establish itself as the paramount power in China by forcing upon Peking the Twenty-one Demands. Washington, at the insistence of Minister Paul S. Reinsch, offered a measure of diplomatic support to China, and Yüan was able to persuade Japan to withdraw the most objectionable of the demands.

Ever since his appointment by Woodrow Wilson, Reinsch had sought to promote American trade and investment in China. At best he had enjoyed mixed success, because American investors had found fairer fields and greater political stability elsewhere. Nonetheless, tepid support from home did not dampen the spirit with which he confronted encroachments upon American rights in China. In this regard, Japan quickly became Reinsch's principal opponent.

After Yüan's demise in 1916, Japan sought to purchase influence in China by subsidizing the warlord Tuan Ch'i-jui in his effort to take power. Reinsch did not believe Japan's explanations that loans and arms shipments to Tuan were intended to create a force to fight for the Allies in France during World War I. Rather, he viewed this Japanese assistance as merely another attempt by Tokyo to gain control over Peking.

Most diplomatic historians have focused on the formation of the Second Banking Consortium as the primary weapon the United States wielded to thwart Japan's aspirations in China.[9] Matsuda Takeshi has provided a most cogent and concise presentation of this thesis. Takeshi noted that Britain, France, and Russia could not restrain Tokyo's initiatives because secret wartime agreements, as well as the Anglo-Japanese alliance, had "deprived them of diplomatic leverage."[10] The United States, however, "rather untied diplomatically, was the only nation which stood in a position to restrain and challenge Japan. The State Department adopted the new Chinese Consortium policy, one of the important objectives of which was to roll back

Japan's wartime advance and secure for the Americans an important voice in the work of modernizing China."[11] As a result of this concentration on the Consortium, historians have largely ignored the crucial role that the China arms embargo, which was imposed in May 1919, concurrently played in limiting Japan's Chinese aspirations.[12]

Washington's willingness to participate in the China arms embargo represented a relatively new departure for the United States. Before 1905, when Theodore Roosevelt imposed an arms embargo over the Dominican Republic, citizens of the United States regularly sold arms to any buyer. Only exceptional circumstances, such as time of war or shortage during a national crisis, dictated an interruption of the export of arms. Furthermore, the United States did not regulate arms sales either to recognized governments or to revolutionary factions. For example, in 1885 and 1891, Washington informed the Colombian and Chilean governments respectively that it could not prevent arms sales to revolutionaries within their borders.[13]

Roosevelt's embargo of the Dominican arms trade departed from this established practice of impartiality, and specifically assisted a Dominican government that faced revolution. In order to weaken the rebels, promote economic stability, and protect lives and property, Washington permitted only the Dominican government to import arms from the United States. To enforce the embargo, the U.S. Navy detained all other shipments to the country.

Critics charged that Roosevelt had not only broken a long-standing tradition, but that the president needed congressional authorization to take this unprecedented action. Roosevelt, however, had an effective response; Congress had issued a joint resolution at the start of the Spanish-American War empowering the president to prohibit the export of war materials, thereby preventing at that time treasonous trade with Spain or its territories from any seaport of the United States. Significantly, this resolution had not been repealed after the conflict ended, and thus Roosevelt was able to resurrect it for use in a way calculated to support the Dominican government against its domestic opponents.[14]

Five years later President William Howard Taft initially chose not to continue Roosevelt's policy regarding arms embargoes. When first confronted with the Mexican Revolution in 1910-1911, Taft refused to honor the request of dictator Porfirio Diaz that the United States end the flow of arms from Texas to revolutionaries in northern Mexico.[15] After Diaz's fall in March 1912, however, Taft reversed himself and embargoed shipments to

Mexico at the request of the newly elected president Francisco Madero. But because the 1898 law could not be used to restrict the arms traffic across the Mexican-U.S. border, Taft needed new legislation. On 14 March 1912, Congress complied, declaring:

Whenever the President shall find that in any American country conditions of domestic violence exist which are promoted by the use of arms or munitions of war procured from the United States, and shall make proclamation thereof, it shall be unlawful to export except under such limitations and exceptions as the President shall prescribe any arms or munitions of war from any place in the United States to such country until otherwise ordered by the President or by Congress.[16]

Within two weeks of proclaiming a total embargo, however, Taft, who was favorably disposed toward the Madero administration, resumed shipments to Madero's forces.[17] In this instance, such blatant partiality in favor of Madero not only led to rebel reprisals against American citizens in Mexico, but it did not prevent Madero's overthrow and subsequent execution in February 1913. Madero's death outraged President Woodrow Wilson and he reinstated the total embargo on arms shipments to Mexico, hoping that this would weaken General Victoriano Huerta's government. Unfortunately the embargo was not only ineffective, but counterproductive; Huerta was able to receive arms from Europe, while his opponents, who controlled no Mexican ports, could not.

Thus both the partial embargo in favor of the Madero government and the total embargo against the Huerta government failed as instruments of U.S. foreign policy. Wilson therefore cancelled the embargo on 3 February 1914 in order to allow the rebel forces of General Venustiano Carranza to obtain American weapons to overthrow Huerta.[18] Mexico was thus left free "to determine her own affairs by domestic force and then by domestic counsel."[19] Except for the period between April and September 1914, when arms shipments were again embargoed to protect American troops occupying Vera Cruz, the United States did not embargo arms to Mexico until October 1915, at that time in support of the Carranza government against its domestic opponents.

By the end of World War I, then, the United States had established the use of an arms embargo as a tool of foreign policy with two uses. On a humanitarian level, an embargo could be used in an attempt to lower the intensity of civil strife by denying war materials to contending factions, thereby protecting lives and property. On a political level, an embargo could be used as a means either to support or to pressure a foreign government. In the Dominican Republic and Mexican cases, however, the United States, for the most part, acted unilaterally; proximity, the extent of American interests, and even the Monroe Doctrine dictated that Washington's decisions would be decisive on questions pertaining to an arms embargo. With the China arms embargo from 1919 to 1929, however, Washington would have no such luxury and instead had to try to achieve through diplomatic channels what it had previously attempted to accomplish on its own.

On 5 May 1919 the powers with diplomatic representatives in China announced that they had "agreed effectively to restrain their subjects and citizens from exporting to or importing into China arms and munitions of war."[20] The U.S. role in the formation and enforcement of the embargo was crucial in depriving Tuan Ch'i-jui's pro-Japanese regime of the materials necessary to sustain itself. Ultimately the embargo succeeded, for in July 1920, Tuan's Japanese-trained and -armed forces were defeated and his government collapsed.

In spite of the success of the China arms embargo, only three scholars have studied it in any detail, and no one has attempted to place it into the larger context of U.S. foreign policy. Elton Atwater devoted a chapter to the embargo in his *American Regulation of Arms Exports*. His treatment, however, is handicapped by an almost exclusive reliance on U.S. government sources.[21] More recently, Noel Pugach provided an excellent analysis of one facet of the embargo in his "Anglo-American Aircraft Competition and the China Arms Embargo, 1919-1921."[22] To date the only monograph available is Anthony Chan's *Arming the Chinese: the Western Armaments Trade in Warlord China, 1920-1928*. Chan had first offered his opinion of the embargo in his dissertation, in which he argued that "the arms embargo agreement of May 5, 1919 was a sham. It was an unqualified failure."[23] Although Chan did not refer to the embargo as a "sham" in his subsequent book, he revealed his opinion of the agreement by concentrating almost exclusively on the mechanics of the armaments trade to China during the life of the embargo.

While Tuan's fall from power was a success for the United States, unfortunately it did not facilitate the formation of a unified national government in China, which was the ostensible goal of the embargo. Washington thus found that the embargo was not merely a short-term policy aimed at the Japanese, but also a long-term commitment to the principle of international cooperation. Historians such as Akira Iriye have generally viewed the Washington Conference (1921-1922) as a harbinger of this new approach to Far Eastern diplomacy: "It was felt that a cooperative framework of action was best suited to maintain the new system of multilateral treaties worked out at the Washington Conference. In the official American conception, the major 'Washington powers' were to co-operate in promoting the evolution of an independent China."[24] Actually, the United States and the other powers had formalized this cooperative policy with the China arms embargo in May of 1919. Ultimately, however, Washington's commitment to this principle waned as enforcement of the embargo proved to be frustrating, and as Americans sought a return to their traditional policy of aloofness in international affairs. Nevertheless, at the very least the arms embargo had benefited the United States by thwarting Japan's hegemonic ambitions in China, the job for which the policy had been designed. The question to be answered in the 1920s was whether or not the embargo would foster conditions in China that would facilitate the unification of the country under pro-Western leadership.

NOTES

1. Alfred Thayer Mahan, *The Problem of Asia* (London: 1900) and Charles Conant, *The United States in the Orient* (Boston: 1900; repr., Port Washington, N.Y.: 1971).

2. Tyler Dennett, *Americans in Eastern Asia* (New York: 1922) and A. Whitney Griswold, *The Far Eastern Policy of the United States* (New Haven: 1938).

3. Dexter Perkins, *America and Two Wars* (Boston: 1944) and Walter Lippmann, *United States Foreign Policy: Shield of the Republic* (Boston: 1943).

4. See for example John King Fairbank, *The United States and China*, 4th ed. (Cambridge, Mass.: 1979).

5. See William Appleman Williams, *The Tragedy of American Diplomacy*, 2nd ed. (New York: 1972), Walter LaFeber, *The New Empire* (Ithaca: 1963), Thomas McCormick, *China Market* (Chicago: 1967), and Eric Foner, *Spanish-Cuban-American War and the Birth of American Imperialism* (New York: 1972). It should be noted, however, that in spite of Washington's defense of the Open Door, American capital was relatively reluctant to enter China both before and after World War I. In 1914, the United States had $49.3 million invested in China, and $196.8 million in 1931. As a percentage

of the total foreign investment in China, this represented a gain from only 3.1% to 6.1%. In comparison, during this period Great Britain's share remained approximately constant at 37%, with investments of $607.5 million in 1914 and $1.19 billion in 1931. The growth of Japan's Chinese investment was most spectacular: from $219.6 million (or 13.6%) in 1914 to $1.14 billion (or 35.1%) in 1931. See Charles Remer, *Foreign Investments in China* (New York: 1933), p. 76.

6. Warren Cohen, *America's Response to China* (New York: 1971), and Paul Varg, *The Closing of the Door* (East Lansing, Mich.: 1973).

7. Gavan McCormack commented that "Chinese military politics of this period [1918-1928] are almost infinitely complex, as any student of its interminable wars, shifting alliances, and feuding factions is aware." Gavan McCormack, *Chang Tso-lin in Northeast China, 1911-1928* (Stanford, Calif.: 1977), p. 45. In this book, warlord politics will be discussed only in so far as they had an impact on, or were effected by, the China arms embargo.

8. This situation in the Far East concerned Secretary of State Robert Lansing, who wrote to President Woodrow Wilson early in 1917 that "Japan evidently aims to take advantage of the preoccupation of her allies to obtain control of China. To do this she desires to prevent all assistance to China from the United States and to keep China weak and divided. . . . I am disposed to believe that the more we yield to Japan the more we shall be asked to yield and that a firm stand upon our undoubted rights will compel modification of Japanese demands upon China." Lansing to Wilson, 17 January 1917, 893.51/1746a, decimal files, United States Department of State, National Archives (hereafter DSNA).

9. See for example Akira Iriye, *Across the Pacific* (New York: 1967), Burton Beers, *Vain Endeavor* (Durham, N.C.: 1962), and Roy Watson Curry, *Woodrow Wilson and Far Eastern Policy* (New York: 1957).

10. Matsuda Takeshi, "Woodrow Wilson's Dollar Diplomacy in the Far East" (Ph.D. diss., University of Wisconsin (Madison), 1979), p. 423.

11. Ibid. Roberta Dayer on page xvi of her *Bankers and Diplomats in China* (London: 1981), gives a revisionist interpretation: "The Second Consortium, which began to take form in 1917, has been treated as a means of halting Japanese wartime loans to Peking. However, in rejoining the Consortium in 1918, the State Department had larger objectives in mind. Rather than protecting China from Japan, the purpose of American diplomacy was to gain control over China's resources."

12. The new Consortium did not come into being until 15 October 1920.

It concluded no loans with China, in part because of Chinese hostility.

13. Secretary of State Thomas Bayard wrote, "The existence of a rebellion in Colombia does not authorize the public officials of the United States to obstruct ordinary commerce in arms between citizens of this country and the rebellious or other parts of the territory of the Republic of Colombia." Bayard to Becerra, 25 March 1885, *Foreign Relations of the United States*, 1885, document 182, p. 238 (hereafter cited as FRUS, followed by the appropriate year. Unless otherwise indicated, all references are to volume 1). See also Bayard to Becerra, 27 March 1885, FRUS 1885, 183, pp. 238-39. With respect to Chile, Secretary of State James G. Blaine wrote, "The laws of the United States on the subject of neutrality . . . do not forbid the manufacture and sale of arms or munitions of war. I am therefore at a loss to find any authority for attempting to forbid the sale and shipment of arms and munitions of war in this country, since such sale and shipment are permitted by our law." Blaine to Lazcano, 13 March 1891, FRUS 1891, unnumbered, p. 314.

14. Elton Atwater, *American Regulation of Arms Exports* (Washington, D.C.: 1941), pp. 37-43.

15. Secretary of State Philander Knox wrote to the Mexican ambassador, "The mere traffic in arms and ammunition by citizens of the United States and Mexico is not forbidden by the rules either of international law or of the neutrality statutes of the United States." Knox to the Mexican Ambassador, 24 January 1911, 812.00/633, FRUS 1911, pp. 396-97.

16. As quoted in Atwater, p. 53.

17. Huntington Wilson to the Mexican Ambassador, 26 March 1912, 812.113/236, FRUS 1912, pp. 765-66.

18. Proclamation by Wilson, 3 February 1914, 812.113/3105a, FRUS 1914, pp. 447-48.

19. Bryan circular telegram, 31 January 1914, 812.00/10735a, FRUS 1914, p. 447.

20. Reinsch to Lansing, 10 May 1919, 693.119/273 FRUS 19, pp. 669-70.

21. Atwater's interpretation is also occasionally flawed. For example, in note 4 on page 123, he remarked that "although Russia was mentioned in the [embargo] agreement of May 5, 1919, she apparently never gave effect to it, and late in the 1920s definitely refused to adhere to it." Here Atwater failed to take into account that a representative of the exiled provisional government of Russia signed the embargo agreement and that the Soviet government did not feel obligated to honor it during the 1920s.

A Policy Calculated to Benefit China

22. Noel Pugach, "Anglo-American Aircraft Competition and the China Arms Embargo, 1919-1921," *Diplomatic History* 2 (Fall 1978): 351-71.

23. Anthony Chan, "Chinese Warlords and the Western Armaments Trade, 1920-1928" (Ph.D. diss., York University (Canada), 1980), p. 143. See also his *Arming the Chinese: The Western Armaments Trade in Warlord China, 1920-1928* (Vancouver: 1982), p. 65.

24. Iriye, *Across the Pacific*, p. 151. On page 12 of her classic work *American Policy and the Chinese Revolution, 1925-1928* (New York: 1947), Dorothy Borg wrote that "the so-called co-operative policy of the Powers in China . . . received the blessing of the Washington Conference."

"A Policy Calculated to Benefit China"

1

Japan's Wartime Gains in China

Minister Paul S. Reinsch, one of the principal architects of the China arms embargo, began his tenure in Peking in 1913 with strong convictions about the proper role the United States should play in Chinese affairs. During the decades before World War I, Great Britain, Japan, Germany, and France had established spheres of influence in China, which Reinsch viewed as detrimental to American as well as Chinese interests. Reinsch opposed European imperialism and colonialism, believing that the world, and especially China, should be open to American trade, capital, and ideas. Indeed, one scholar concluded that Reinsch was "obsessed with the need to find foreign outlets for America's surplus goods and capital."[1]

Reinsch brought to China a potent vision of the Open Door policy, and toiled ceaselessly to promote American trade and investment in that country, believing it would benefit both parties. Unfortunately Reinsch's repeated efforts fell victim to Chinese politics, foreign interference, and to cautious American businessmen who were reluctant to play the role he assigned them. But disappointment did not lead Reinsch to reevaluate his fundamental views, and the lack of progress only spurred him on. Even after he resigned his position in the wake of the Versailles Peace Conference, he continued to lobby for China in the United States as a paid representative of the Chinese government. Until his death in 1923, he steadfastly maintained that both Americans and Chinese would find solutions to their problems through the large-scale investment of American capital in China.[2]

Woodrow Wilson's administration did not discourage Reinsch's efforts in Peking. The president revealed his own sympathies to the cabinet in the opening days of his first term: "I feel so keenly the desire to help China that I prefer to err in the line of helping that country than otherwise."[3]   But ultimately Wilson was either unwilling or unable to translate these sympathies into strong policy; from the outset his administration, confronted with turmoil in Mexico, forced to focus increasingly on issues arising from World War I, and obviously concerned with domestic politics, was too preoccupied elsewhere to devote much attention to China.[4] And even when Chinese affairs demanded action by the United States, the opinions of foreign governments, especially London and Tokyo, necessarily influenced Washington's views.

Great Britain had established a predominant position in China over the course of little more than two generations. From their base in the Yangtze River Valley, the British had the lion's share of China's foreign trade and investment. London, therefore, had no desire to see any change in the status quo as a result of either Chinese domestic unrest or foreign encroachment. Furthermore the voice of the British minister, Sir John Jordan, carried great weight in Peking's diplomatic and political circles; he was the key European figure in China until he retired from the foreign service in 1920.[5]

While Great Britain strove to maintain its position in China, officials in the Japanese military and government believed that events in China were crucial to Japan's future prosperity. Japan's victorious wars against China in 1894-1895 and Russia in 1904-1905 had won it the right to compete in the great game of empire in the Far East with the other powers. While Japan's overall ambitions in China varied according to circumstances, its interest in Manchuria remained paramount. Japan had established its position in the Three Eastern Provinces at the cost of "one hundred thousand soldiers' blood" during the Russo-Japanese War and had subsequently invested more than $1 billion there in order to develop the region and exploit its resources.[6]

Although bound together by a defensive alliance after 1902, London and Tokyo frequently worked at cross-purposes in China. No better example of this occurred than World War I, which dramatically altered the balance of power in the Far East. War eliminated the Germans and Russians as major participants; even more significantly, the British (and also the French), locked in a life or death struggle with Germany, were forced to defer to the wishes of their Japanese ally.[7] As Iriye has remarked, Tokyo sought to exploit this unprecedented opportunity without delay:

The European war seemed a heaven-sent opportunity to entrench and solidify Japanese influence on the continent of Asia so as to prevent Western powers from overwhelming Japanese interests. Because of the notion that the nation was not entirely accepted as an equal, bold action seemed needed to take advantage of the West's distress so that its postwar counteroffensive would not materialize. This was the psychological background of the Twenty-one Demands negotiations, schemes to detach Manchuria and Mongolia from China, the "Nishihara loans," the tranfer of German rights in Shantung to Japan, and other policies and machinations pursued during the war.[8]

Ironically Reinsch (and Secretary of State Robert Lansing) also viewed the war as providing an excellent opportunity for the United States in China. But Reinsch, in spite of the fact that he spoke with the backing of the State Department, had little success convincing businessmen that this was the case. Fears of international (especially Japanese) objections and anxiety about the security of any investment in China led American firms to turn a deaf ear to Reinsch's and Washington's requests for private financial assistance.[9]

But the Japanese government of Prime Minister Okuma Shigenobu soon gave Reinsch a graver concern than that of timid American capital. On 18 January 1915, Japan presented Yüan Shih-k'ai with the Twenty-one Demands, a package assembled by Foreign Minister Kato Komei to settle pending issues between the two countries. Kato, however, had an even grander scheme in mind. The fifth group of demands included provisions for joint Sino-Japanese administration of police forces, and virtually nullified Chinese sovereignty. It would have entrenched Tokyo's preponderant influence in Peking. The demands were so extreme that some Western officials were hesitant to give credence to the first Chinese accounts of them.[10]

Reinsch sounded the alarm in a series of telegrams to Washington. He did not believe that Tokyo was merely pursuing either a temporary advantage in China or a larger share of the Chinese pie than the Western powers had previously allowed. Instead, he saw the demands as the opening stage of Japan's desire to dominate the Far East.[11] Reinsch advised the Chinese to prolong the negotiations with Japan over the Twenty-one Demands as long as possible and at the same time to appeal to world opinion for support. This strategy was partially successful, for the Japanese withdrew the demands that had most greatly infringed on China's sovereignty.

The Twenty-one Demands episode clearly betrayed the extent of Japan's Chinese aspirations and helped generate two forces that in part resulted in the China arms embargo four years later. On the one hand the British began to re-think their Far Eastern policy, which depended on the Anglo-Japanese alliance to defend the Empire's interests; after 1915 London increasingly sought the assistance of the United States in curbing the ambitions of

Tokyo.[12]   On the other hand, in Washington, the Wilson administration became more determined to prevent an expansion of Japan's influence in China. Reinsch needed no particular prompting from the State Department in this regard. He was a determined foe of Japan, convinced of the necessity of keeping a close watch on Tokyo's machinations.[13]

Reinsch's vigilance was justified, because the Japanese were determined to dominate Chinese affairs. Even before the Twenty-one Demands, Japan had viewed Yüan's government with misgiving, in part because of the personal friendship between Yüan and Sir John Jordan.[14] This animosity toward Yüan mounted in the wake of his attempt to thwart the Twenty-one Demands. Aware of Japan's hostility towards his regime, Yüan strove to shore up his position vis-à-vis Tokyo in any way he could.[15] Some scholars have viewed Yüan's monarchical scheme of 1915 as a weapon to foil external threats and build domestic strength.[16] But Yüan miscalculated. Ultimately, a combination of foreign pressure as well as republican agitation within China forced him to abandon his scheme and to resign his office by the middle of 1916.

In the months preceding Yüan's fall from power, Reinsch grew anxious over China's future. He did not restrain his sentiments regarding who was to blame for the troubled state of affairs: "As the Japanese have so much to gain from disturbances and unrest in China, it is quite natural that public belief should credit them with widespread and active intrigue, for which, indeed, past experience offers precedents and towards which a large number of isolated details point."[17] In contrast, as late as March 1916 Jordan was able to wax philosophical on the course of events: "The standard of morality amongst Nations in their intercourse with each other is not particularly high at any time and is apt to degenerate in times like the present when there is world wide confusion. Japan can, therefore, hardly be blamed for exploiting the present situation in China."[18]   Within a month, however, Jordan's opinions changed after conditions in China had deteriorated sharply. Trade, which had flourished for the previous two years, was at a standstill, and chaos reigned at Canton and other ports. At this juncture, Jordan wrote "the debacle is now upon us . . . [because of] this mad Monarchist scheme and the skillful use that has been made of it."[19] Yet beyond the disruption of trade and the potential end to the punctual payment of foreign obligations, Jordan did not yet express marked hostility to Japan for causing this state of affairs. He merely observed at the beginning of May 1916 that "once the present Chinese Government disappears, there is likely to be a general scramble and a hopeless mess."[20]

Reinsch did not believe that the United States could view China's chaos with such equanimity, lest it allow Tokyo to slam shut the Open Door.[21] At the end of May 1916 he repeated his accusations that Japanese nationals were participating in the revolutionary movement against Yüan, and that they did so under the protective shield of Japanese authorities. Furthermore, he warned that the only "absolutely definite principle" of Japanese policy seemed to be that Yüan must be ousted regardless of the cost involved.[22] Reinsch warned Washington that should this be accomplished it might be taken for granted in Tokyo that the prestige of Japan had been greatly increased and that any successor to Yüan would necessarily feel his dependence on the Japanese government.[23] Reinsch's remarks proved prescient. From the ruins of Yüan's government, Tuan Ch'i-jui emerged to become premier in 1916. His military record, personal integrity, and opposition to Yüan's monarchial scheme, made him, at least initially, acceptable to the various factions in China.[24] Ultimately he was also acceptable to officials in the Japanese army and government, who after the summer of 1917 sought to establish Tuan as their client in Peking.

For their part the Japanese did not soft-pedal the extensive role they could play in Chinese domestic politics. For example, Minister Hioki Eki received instructions to warn Tuan that a continuation of Yüan's anti-Japanese policy would be a cause for concern in Tokyo. Hioki also promised that if Tuan did not continue Yüan's policies, he could expect aid from Japan.[25]

Tuan's recognition of Japan's predominant position in the Far East did not prevent him, at least initially, from trying to make a deal with the United States. But as Reinsch's promises of assistance fell short of Chinese expectations, Tuan relied more and more on his pro-Japanese advisers who had personal contacts in high Tokyo circles.[26] Nowhere was this more true than in the realm of public finance, because internal disorder had disrupted the usual revenues of the central government and compelled Peking to seek foreign loans. Since World War I dried up the flow of capital from Europe, the Chinese had to look either to American or Japanese banks for funds. Recognizing the political gain to be made as Peking's sole source of foreign money, the Japanese endeavored to prevent American loans to China. Towards this end they resorted to obstructive tactics such as diplomatic pressure, a publicity campaign in the American press, and the offering of loans on better terms.[27]

In addition to discouraging the flow of American capital into China, the Japanese were also old hands at "yen diplomacy," particularly in their Manchurian sphere of interest. The American consul-general at Mukden reported in despair one such example to Reinsch shortly after the start of World War I:

> It is a pity that the government here can not be prevented from dissipating, through reckless and unchecked borrowing, Manchuria's tangible securities. One need have no hesitancy in predicting with a feeling of positive assurance that the property affording the security of this loan, the Penhsihu Colliery and Mining Company, will at the expiration of the period of this loan, i.e. two years, pass completely and permanently into the hands of the Japanese.[28]

Furthermore, not only did Japan accrue political advantage from having made these loans (and could expect the economic benefit of acquiring Chinese properties when the loans were defaulted), but the advances themselves were usually hedged with conditions that invariably returned the proceeds to the Japanese.[29] By early 1917 the new U.S. consul-general at Mukden went so far as to speculate that "as almost every available security here is hypothecated to the Japanese, and other foreign loans are practically out of the question, and as the local government is already in financial straits, the day is probably not far off when Japan will appoint itself a sort of receiver to manage the affairs of the Manchurian government."[30] To a larger degree, during the two years preceding the end of World War I, the Japanese attempted to practice the methods perfected in Mukden and Manchuria in Peking and China.

In this regard some Japanese had recognized that Okuma Shigenobu's earlier sledgehammer diplomacy, as evidenced in the Twenty-one Demands, was counterproductive because of the anti-Japanese sentiments it fueled in China as well as in the West. When Terauchi Masatake replaced Okuma as prime minister in October 1916, he appointed to his cabinet men highly critical of his predecessor's foreign policy. Terauchi did not, however, quarrel with Okuma's goal of establishing close ties between Japan and China. Terauchi would change Japan's means, not ends, with respect to China.[31]

At the very outset, Terauchi's government declared that it would pursue a policy of noninterference in Chinese affairs. At the same time, however, the cabinet decided to make use of the large supply of capital Japan had acquired as a result of the country's expanded wartime trade with the West. This capital, which went to China in the form of the so-called Nishihara loans, was ostensibly designated to promote Chinese railroad construction and general economic development. But actually the loans were made solely for political purposes.[32]

To implement this policy of economic imperialism, the Japanese soon found a willing client within Tuan's cabinet. Ts'ao Ju-lin, the minister of communications, accepted a Japanese loan of five million yen to the Bank of Communications in January of 1917.[33] In reporting the conclusion of this first Nishihara loan to Washington, Reinsch lamented:

> It appears that the Japanese have finally found an ally in China who has both unusual ability and official experience, in the person of Mr. Ts'ao Ju-lin, ex-Vice Minister for Foreign Affairs. . . . Until recently, he has, however, taken a national Chinese stand, i.e. that while believing in friendly relations with the Japanese, he did not appear willing to give Japanese agencies a prominent place in Chinese affairs. He seems to have changed now.[34]

But Reinsch did not despair. In spite of the growing influence Ts'ao Ju-lin's so-called communications clique enjoyed because of its access to Japanese funds, Reinsch did not believe that Tuan had yet committed himself to the Japanese.[35]

Washington soon provided Reinsch with what he believed was a golden opportunity to rescue China from Japan. In early February 1917 the United States broke diplomatic relations with Germany after Berlin resumed unrestricted submarine warfare, and Washington asked other neutral nations to join in this American protest. Initially Tuan gave a sympathetic hearing to Reinsch's request that the Chinese associate themselves with the United States, because Tuan still hoped to check Japan by allying China with another power.[36]

But ultimately Reinsch's plan to use China's entrance into World War I under American auspices as a means to neutralize Japanese influence backfired disastrously.[37] Washington undermined Reinsch's credibility with the Chinese by its unwillingness to make good on his premature promise of American support for a Chinese declaration of war. Furthermore Tuan had miscalculated the depth of the domestic opposition against entering the conflict. His opponents, based primarily in southern China, feared that Tuan would use the war to entrench himself and his northern warlord allies more firmly in power. Tuan's opponents, both within and outside of the Chinese parliament, united against him and he was forced from office in May 1917.[38]

Tuan's fall, however, did not end the affair. Tokyo now also desired Chinese participation in the war, albeit under Japanese rather than American tutelage. By the end of May, the pro-intervention military governors under Japanese influence (in Manchuria, Shantung, and Anhui) threatened to cut their ties to the Peking government unless the anti-war Parliament were dissolved.[39] Reinsch had managed to maneuver the United States into an embarrassing position because these pro-intervention, pro-Japanese militarists had "succeeded as to have created the general belief that their movement has the tacit approval of the Powers at war with Germany."[40] Such a situation was obviously not in the interest of the United States, so on 4 June Lansing informed Peking, as well as London, Paris, and Tokyo, that Washington considered China's entry into the war a secondary consideration "as compared with [the] unity and peace of China."[41]

From the British legation, Chargé d'Affaires Beilby Alston wrote that he and his principal colleagues in Peking believed that Reinsch had made a bad "gaffe." Although otherwise considering Reinsch "quite a good creature," he was of the opinion that the American minister "has not been able to resist the temptation to dabble in Chinese politics, which comes to most *amateur* [emphasis added] diplomatists in the Far East." Alston believed that Reinsch should have waited for at least six months before making his initiative, thereby allowing U.S. military forces to improve Washington's diplomatic position before attempting a scheme so damaging to the Allied cause.[42]

Reinsch briefly believed that his plan to have China enter World War I was not a total failure. In July 1917 General Chang Hsün installed Pu Yi as emperor and attempted to restore the Manchu empire; to meet the crisis, President Li Yüan-hung reappointed Tuan premier as well as commander-in-chief, and the restoration movement collapsed. Tuan entered Peking on 13 July as the savior of the republic with his political prestige greatly enhanced.[43] In spite of Tuan's continued reliance on pro-Japanese advisers, Reinsch still expressed confidence in his abilities. In early October he stated that "the strength of General Tuan lies . . . not so much in constructive ability or knowledge of men or administrative talent, in all of which he is not deemed eminent, but in wisdom and honesty of purpose."[44] But Reinsch ultimately changed his opinion because Tuan returned to power determined to crush his domestic opposition and to unite the country by force. Anti-Tuan elements fled southward and in Canton on 1 September 1917 they established the National Military Government under the nominal leadership of Sun Yat-sen. Reinsch had therefore helped initiate the chain of events which ultimately resulted in the formal division of China into two warring factions.[45] For all of the powers, this division would lead to years of economic and political instability in their China markets. For the United States and Great Britain in particular, it portended a renewed Japanese assault on Chinese sovereignty.

NOTES

1. Noel Pugach, *Paul S. Reinsch: Open Door Diplomat in Action* (Millwood, N.Y.: 1979), p. 74. See also p. 40.

2. Ibid., pp. 77, 116. See also Patrick Scanlan, "No Longer a Treaty Port: Paul S. Reinsch and China, 1913-1919" (Ph.D. diss., University of Wisconsin (Madison), 1973), pp. 5, 371-73.

3. E. David Cronon, ed., *The Cabinet Diaries of Josephus Daniels* (Lincoln, Neb.: 1963), entry for 28 March 1913, p. 17.

4. Pugach, *Reinsch,* p. 74.

5. Donald Dignan, *New Perspectives on British Far Eastern Policy* (Brisbane: 1969), p. 269.

6. Akira Iriye, *After Imperialism* (Cambridge, Mass.: 1965), p. 111.

7. In this regard, a 1916 letter from Jordan to Lord Bryce is instructive: "You will, of course, realize that our position in China has been an extremely delicate one during the past eighteen months and we have been obliged to live largely upon the prestige acquired in the past. Our action has necessarily been adapted to the circumstances and not what it would have been in normal circumstances." Sir John Jordan to Lord Bryce, 23 February 1916, British Government Documents, Foreign Office File 350 volume 15, Public Record Office, London [hereafter references to the Foreign Office records at the PRO will be cited by the F.O. volume and the document file number if given]. Reinsch reported to Washington that the "Japanese utilize the alliance [with Great Britain] for the purpose of independent action of the European Allies and to force them to follow Japan's lead." Reinsch to Lansing, 27 May 1917, 893.51/3009, DSNA.

8. Iriye, *Across the Pacific,* p. 132. Japan was also not above allowing rumors of a Japanese-German rapprochement to circulate, so as to force the Allies to accede to further Japanese demands during the war. See Pugach, *Reinsch*, p. 144.

9. Scanlan, pp. 221-22. Eventually Reinsch cast most of the blame for this failure on American businessmen, whom he believed timid, shortsighted, backward in their techniques, ignorant of China, and indifferent to the

promotion of U.S. national interests abroad. See Pugach, *Reinsch*, p. 169.

10. Ernest Young, *The Presidency of Yüan Shih-K'ai* (Ann Arbor, Mich.: 1977), p. 188.

11. Pugach, *Reinsch*, p. 148. See also, FRUS 1915, pp. 118-24.

12. Dayer, p. 41. See also Peter Lowe, *Great Britain and Japan, 1911-1915* (London: 1969), pp. 255-58.

13. Beers, p. 36. Pugach, *Reinsch*, p. 157. The views of John Van Antwerp MacMurray (a junior member of the legation who later became minister at Peking) were best expressed in a letter to his mother: "I do feel that if the United States and Great Britain (particularly the former) so adhere to pacific counsels as to be unwilling to make any representations to Japan, the result will eventually be to force one or both of us to bear the brunt of war with Japan, if not in this Administration, in some future one." John Van Antwerp MacMurray to his mother, 13 February 1915, John Van Antwerp MacMurray Papers, Library of Congress, box 48. (hereafter cited as MacMurray Papers).

14. Soon after Yüan's death, Jordan wrote to Sir Walter Langley, "As to Yüan Shih-k'ai, you will not expect a balanced opinion from me at the moment. I had a great personal liking for the man and feel both his loss and the manner of it acutely. . . . I could go on indefinitely reciting acts to the credit of my dead friend--for simply as a friend I shall always remember him." Jordan to Langley, 13 June 1916, F.O. 350/15, PRO.

15. Hsi-ping Shao, "From the Twenty-one Demands to the Sino-Japanese Military Agreements," in Alvin Coox and Hilary Conroy, eds. *China and Japan* (Santa Barbara, Calif. : 1978), p. 38.

16. Ernest Young, p. 220. Young stated that "the aftermath of the Twenty-one Demands produced not a confidence that the Japanese would support him [Yüan] in whatever he did, but a desperate lunge at an institutional alteration that might help to protect him against them."

17. Reinsch to Lansing, 24 February 1916, 893.00/2363, FRUS 1916, p. 62.

18. Jordan prefaced this remark saying, "There will be no peace in China so long as the European War lasts, and the longer it continues, the more precarious will be the position of any Government which attempts to rule this country." Jordan to Langley, 14 March 1916, F.O. 350/15, PRO.

19. Jordan to Langley, 16 April 1916, F.O. 350/15, PRO. Jordan also lamented that, "With all its faults, and they were legion, I am afraid it will be some time before we get an Administration which will be an improvement upon that of Yüan Shih-k'ai."

20. Jordan to Langley, 1 May 1916, F.O. 350/15, PRO. On 29 June he

commented to Langley that "this war has stirred up the dry bones of Asia and I expect the aftermath will raise serious problems for us." On 20 July he was even more exact: "If I am not mistaken, Asiatic problems will follow closely upon the heels of a European settlement." See Jordan to Langley, 29 June and 20 July 1916, F.O. 350/15, PRO.

21. He reported to Washington that "responsible Chinese as well as Europeans look upon American assistance as the last resort of Chinese independence and of international rights in China." Reinsch to Lansing, 27 May 1917, 893.51/3009, DSNA.

22. Reinsch to Lansing, 31 May 1916, 893.00/2442, FRUS 1916, p. 83.

23. Ibid. Reinsch's estimations of Japanese policy were accurate; Ernest Young wrote that "on March 7 the Japanese cabinet for the first time made the removal of Yüan a formal objective. . . . The cabinet also held that Japan should not exceed the limits of tolerance of the European powers and the United States regarding interference in Chinese affairs. But quiet infusion of money into the rebellion . . . [was] deemed appropriate." Ernest Young, p. 240.

24. Shao, p. 41.

25. Madeleine Chi, *China Diplomacy* (Cambridge, Mass.: 1970), p. 84.

26. Shao, p. 45.

27. Takeshi, p. 143.

28. Heintzleman to Reinsch, 15 October 1914, 893.51/1548, DSNA. For an almost identical report two years later, see 30 June 1916, 893.51/1669, DSNA.

29. Heintzleman to Reinsch, 16 August 1916, 893.51/1689, DSNA.

30. Baker to Reinsch, 30 January 1917, 893.51/1762, DSNA.

31. Beers, pp. 79-80.

32. Dayer, p. 42. Madeleine Chi, "Ts'ao Ju-lin: His Japanese Connection," in Iriye, *The Chinese and Japanese,* pp. 145-47. Such policies were apparently successful, for by the fall of 1917 the American commercial attaché at Peking reported to Washington that the "Opportunities for American commercial enterprises in China [are] seriously threatened by [the] aggressive attitude of Japan to China [which is] destined, if not curbed, to place China under Japanese political domination and through the control of the valuable natural resources irreparably to injure American interests." Arnold to the Secretary of Commerce, 26 October 1917, 893.51/1823, DSNA.

33. Pugach, *Reinsch,* p. 214. During 1917 and 1918, eight Nishihara loans totaling about 145 million yen (approximately $72.5 million) were extended to

Tuan's regime. See Fairbank, *Cambridge History of China*, vol. 13, pt. 1, p. 102.

34. Reinsch to Lansing, 26 Jan 1917, 893.00/2565, DSNA. Reinsch soon passed an unfavorable judgment on the effect of such influence: "The state of affairs is not encouraging. General dissatisfaction prevails partly because of unprecedented official corruption, lack of policy and authority; partly because of [the] great influence of [the] Japanese clique over the Government." Reinsch to Lansing, 26 March 1917, 893.00/2567, DSNA.

35. Reinsch to Lansing, 14 June 1917, 893.00/2675, DSNA.

36. Shao, p. 43.

37. Pugach, *Reinsch,* p. 232.

38. Shao, p. 46. Commenting on the state of affairs in Peking during this crisis, MacMurray wrote that "things are in a terrible whirl here: the Chinese Government is about as completely disorganized as any institution could be; it is not just a matter of differences between parties,--it's an utter confusion and demoralization, in which everyone concerned is dodging responsibility and letting things take care of themselves." MacMurray to his mother, 23 May 1917, MacMurray Papers, box 55.

39. Reinsch to Lansing, 30 May 1917, 893.00/2579, FRUS 1917, pp. 47-48. See also Reinsch to Lansing, 2 June 1917, 893.00/2581, FRUS 1917, p. 48.

40. Reinsch to Lansing, 6 June 1917, 893.00/2588, FRUS 1917, p. 55.

41. See Lansing to Sharp, 4 June 1917, 893.00/2581, FRUS 1917, p. 49. China declared war on Germany in August 1917.

42. Beilby Alston to Sir Walter Langley, 19 June 1917, Langley Papers, F.O. 800/30, PRO.

43. Shao, p. 46.

44. Reinsch to Lansing, 12 October 1917, 893.00/2736, DSNA.

45. Pugach, *Reinsch*, p. 232-33. Sir John Jordan was led to remark at this time that "this country is now afflicted with a vast mass of disorganized troops ranged under leaders most of whom are fighting for motives of personal ascendancy. It is a fact that 65% of the total revenue of the State is at present being devoted to military purposes and it would probably be a blessing if, as a local writer has humorously suggested, China could drop her military paraphernalia and return to the days of bows and arrows." Jordan to Balfour, 30 October 1917, F.O. 371/3177, 2518, PRO.

2

Japan's Apogee in China

Tuan's political resurrection in the wake of Chang Hsün's restoration fiasco presented the powers with a successful, and for the time being, popular leader within China. But which power would seize the opportunity to try to influence both Tuan and the course of Chinese politics? Ultimately Tokyo acted decisively and forced Washington and London to respond to Japanese initiatives.

With Tuan apparently in firm control of Peking, the Terauchi cabinet decided at the end of July 1917 to offer him diplomatic, economic, and military aid. Furthermore, the Japanese terminated all cooperation with the anti-Peking elements in the south.[1] The goal of this "aid-Tuan" policy was the reunification of China under leadership that recognized its dependence on Japan. The Japanese military, particularly army leaders, wanted Tokyo to undertake this task with all due haste; they correctly foresaw that Japan's window of opportunity in China would soon close, for the United States had declared war on Germany, which portended an end to World War I and a return to Asia by the powers.[2] Tokyo moved quickly; a month after the cabinet's decision, the Japanese concluded a 10 million yen loan to China, and in September, negotiated another loan of 20 million yen.[3]

Needless to say, this fresh extension of Japanese influence disturbed Reinsch and he worked to find an alternate source of funding for Peking. Reinsch tried to convince both the financial community in the United States and his superiors in Washington that funds for China would not be wasted by reporting that the "financial situation of China, considering all circumstances, is good, but a moderate amount of support is essential in order to avoid control of China by Japan."[4] Throughout the year, representatives of various financial groups in the United States undertook negotiations towards the re-formation of an American group to rejoin the six-power banking Consortium in China.   Reinsch presently favored American participation in the Consortium: "Greatly changed circumstances consequent upon the war, carefully considered, appear to impose the conclusion that the participation of the United States in international public finance in China is the best method for preserving the international balance, Chinese national existence and full fruition of American enterprise, educational and economic."[5] Reinsch implied that Japanese influence could be checked and American interests preserved through this international body. He would have preferred an independent loan by the United States to China, and he advocated participation in the Consortium only as a *pis aller* in order to facilitate the flow of non-Japanese funds into the country. If an American or Consortium loan was not forthcoming, he feared that Japan would make more loans on its own.[6]

While American financial negotiations dragged on, however, Nishihara Kamezo negotiated a series of Japanese loans to the Peking government. Strictly speaking, such loans did not make financial sense, because of China's unstable internal condition.[7]   But from Tokyo's perspective, these loans conveyed important political and economic advantages; in return for having made the loans, the Japanese exacted from Peking various concessions, ranging from railroad and mining rights to the appointment of Japanese advisers to the Chinese government.[8]

Although Tuan's government had found a foreign source of money, Tokyo's growing influence in Peking stimulated mounting Chinese resentment toward Japan. As of yet, however, the Chinese themselves were either unable to resist such encroachment, or collaborated with the Japanese. Some form of outside intervention, then, could provide the only check to the Japanese advance. Since World War I effectively eliminated the European powers from the scene for the duration of the conflict, the Japanese had concluded early on that only the United States could limit Japan's Asian aspirations. As the American Chargé d'Affaires in Tokyo, Post Wheeler, remarked in June of 1917: "The belief that the activities of the Legation at Peking were being exerted against Japanese interests and influence in China has been growing here during the past three years. . . . This distrust of our friendliness at Peking, then sufficiently vague [in 1914], has since kept pace with Japan's growing nervousness where China is concerned."[9] In order to preserve Japan's growing investment in China and to prevent possible American interference, Tokyo made several attempts to reach an understanding with the Wilson administration in the latter part of 1917.

The initial approach came on 14 June, with the announcement that Viscount Ishii Kikujiro had been appointed ambassador extraordinary and plenipotentiary in order to conduct high-level negotiations regarding Chinese affairs with the United States. But the day after this indication that Tokyo was willing to discuss the situation with Washington, Lansing reported to Reinsch and Wheeler that the Japanese assumed a more hard-line position:

The Ambassador here on June 15 declared that Japan had special and close relations, political as well as economic with China and that this was recognized by Mr. Bryan when Secretary of State, who had also stated that American activity in China was never political. The Japanese Government requests the American Government to confirm Mr. Bryan's statement and repeat his assurance of a friendly attitude towards Japan in respect to Chinese problems.[10]

Reinsch vigorously opposed the Japanese claim that Bryan had implied in 1915 that China was no longer an independent state and that Japan controlled the diplomatic relations between the United States and China. Reinsch accurately surmised that the Japanese had read more into Bryan's statement than the secretary of state had intended. In March 1915 Bryan had recognized only that Japan's relations with China were "special and close"; Reinsch protested to Lansing that in spite of Japan's declaration to the contrary, "No matter how friendly Mr. Bryan's intentions, he could certainly not have admitted the existence of a Japanese protectorate over China."[11] In his subsequent reply to the Japanese note, Lansing denied that the United States had departed from its traditional China policy and asserted that the United States did not claim for itself, nor "recognize the right or paramount interest of any other country to extend political influence over China."[12]

Undaunted, Tokyo again tried to solidify its position in China after Tuan's return to power in July. In this instance, however, the Japanese employed a more subtle approach. On 9 August the British ambassador to Tokyo, Sir Conyngham Greene, received a confidential memorandum from the Japanese government requesting that Great Britain support the Terauchi cabinet's aid-Tuan policy. The memorandum stated that it was in the interest of the allied powers for China to have a stable government, and that Tuan's government offered a greater prospect in this regard than the southern leadership that opposed him. Therefore, "the interest of the Allies is . . . to support this government who have the courage to declare war against Germany."[13] After London expressed its approval, Tokyo requested British assistance in approaching the United States to solicit Washington's support. London concurred and informed Lansing on 3 September that His Majesty's

Government were "convinced that the adoption by all the Allied Powers of a policy based on these lines affords the best prospect of the restoration of order in China."[14]

The British note, along with the formal Japanese request delivered the next day, placed the United States in an awkward position. On the one hand, for the sake of Allied unity, stability within China, and a potentially more effective prosecution of the war on Peking's part, the United States could accept the Japanese initiative and support a Chinese government already sympathetic to Japan. On the other hand, the United States could accept the diplomatic costs of declining to work with the Allies in support of Tuan's government. Caught on the horns of this dilemma, Lansing attempted to safeguard American interests as best he could. He accepted in principle the views expressed in the Japanese memorandum, including the statement that "the Japanese Government have no intention of showing nor have any reason to show any preference for either of the political factions in China."[15] Lansing, however, was not content to rely solely on Tokyo's word that Japan would abide by its pledge not to interfere in China's internal affairs. In attempting to prevent Japan from exploiting the situation by making unilateral grants of support to the Peking government, Lansing added: "The American government . . . is of the opinion that the principal powers at war with Germany ought at once to confer together and agree upon the best method of supplying [to the Central Government of China] that effective support to which the memorandum . . . [of the Imperial Japanese Government] refers."[16] Thus, the principle of mutual cooperation could possibly be used to check Japan's machinations in China.

This Japanese-British-American agreement did not revise Reinsch's estimation of Tokyo's intentions, and he remained vigilant for signs of fresh Japanese encroachments. Jordan informed London in October 1917 of Reinsch's alarm at recent Sino-Japanese negotiations:

The American Minister . . . who is much concerned at these developments and who has apparently been actively engaged in trying to thwart them, is convinced that a so-called "arms alliance" has virtually been concluded between some members of the Cabinet and unofficial Japanese agents, and that it carries with it the right to nominate a few Japanese advisers, nominally to see that the arms are not used against the south, but in reality to gain a footing for the exercise of eventual control in the military administration of China.[17]

Reinsch as yet retained faith in Premier Tuan, in spite of the activities of some cabinet members. Earlier that same month Reinsch reported to Washington Tuan's "enlightened programme" to remove the army from politics once the country was unified. He believed that Tuan's efforts were sincere and furthermore reported that Tuan's "prestige and the confidence in his integrity are great and have been gaining in strength constantly. . . . Younger men of great ability in the Government, who have little confidence in the power of the old-time leaders to do anything for China, look to General Tuan as the man under whose leadership they would have the greatest opportunity to build up the Government."[18]

Sir John Jordan, however, was much more pessimistic. At the end of October Jordan warned London of his fears that "the Government of this country has largely fallen under Japanese influence, and trusts in a great measure to that influence to see it safely through its struggle with the south."[19] Several officials in the Foreign Office agreed with Jordan, for minuted beneath his telegram were the remarks: "The Japanese have begun to work their 'special interests' with a vengeance"; "The Japanese are certainly becoming economically all powerful in China"; and ominously, "They are the great danger of the future."[20]

Jordan did see a possible solution to the problems posed by the Japanese: "There is an aspect of the situation on which I venture to touch with much diffidence. All this tangle of schemes, concessions, and loans is accentuating the acute local estrangement which exists between Japan and the United States, *and if the views of the American Minister reflect those of his Government* [emphasis added], there is a growing disposition to challenge Japan's action in China."[21] Jordan's insight penetrated to the heart of the matter; if Reinsch and Washington were in agreement, the United States might act at any time to reverse the alarming trend in Chinese affairs. But the State Department and its minister at Peking were not in agreement. In fact, even as Jordan composed his despatch, Lansing and Ishii hammered together a statement on the status of Chinese affairs of which Reinsch would later write, "Instead of support we gave China the Lansing-Ishii note (as interpreted by Japan)."[22]

Reinsch first learned of the agreements not from the State Department, but from the Japanese minister, who informed him that the American government recognized "the special interests of Japan in China."[23] Realizing the potential for mischief in this ambiguous declaration, Reinsch sarcastically asked his government: "While I understand that the reasons which prompted this momentous decision are confidential, I have the honor to ask whether at the time of the publication of this note you desire me to present to the Chinese officials any explanation of this action which so profoundly affects their interests and which at first sight appears a reversal of American policy in China."[24]   Indeed, many Chinese resented the apparent American capitulation to Japanese expansionism. In fact, for once the rival Chinese governments found common ground in condemning the notes: the northern regime in Peking declared that "the Chinese Government will not allow herself to be bound by any agreement entered into by other nations," while the southern regime in Canton attacked the accords as "offending the spirit of American friendly policies toward China."[25]

As one of Reinsch's biographers has noted, perhaps just as significant was the effect the notes had on the minister. Daniel Gage wrote that the affair disheartened Reinsch, who thereafter merely "marked time" in Peking, and concerned himself with reporting, "not with planning definite and positive forward plans to save China for the United States by thwarting Japan." Gage concluded that "no activities and measures as serious as those of 1915-1917 were attempted by Reinsch after the Lansing-Ishii agreement. The day was Japan's. As he witnessed the rapid extension of her financial, political, and military operations in China and its vicinity, Reinsch grew increasingly alarmed, but could do hardly more than sound the alarm. Effective action he could not take."[26]   It is true that the period between the Lansing-Ishii agreements and the end of World War I witnessed the apogee of Japanese influence in Chinese affairs; Reinsch, although disheartened at the lack of support he received from the United States, in December told Lansing that he would nevertheless still endeavor "quietly to preserve our own in this field and to build for the future."[27]   While one can agree with Gage in concluding that Reinsch did not plan "positive forward" steps to save China, he would play a key role in negating Japanese influence through the subsequent institution of the arms embargo and a ban on loans to China.

For the balance of 1917 and through the spring of 1918, Reinsch could do little but witness the course of events in China. Tokyo, having reinforced its position with the Nishihara loans and the Lansing-Ishii notes, now took the aid-Tuan policy one step further with the sale of armaments to the Peking regime. The initial agreement involving nearly 19 million yen worth of material was concluded between the Japanese Taihei Kumiai Consortium and Peking on 30 December 1917. This assistance was to be channeled through the newly created War Participation Bureau, under the direction of none other than General Tuan Ch'i-jui. The Japanese also sought to safeguard their position by stipulating in the arms contract the preferential right of Japan to supply further arms to China, and that Japanese officers would be engaged to train Chinese troops.[28]

This agreement, although ostensibly concluded in order to prepare China for war against Germany, obviously had larger significance within the context of the conflict between Tuan and his southern opponents. Tokyo, sensitive to criticism concerning its China policy, did attempt to allay suspicions with a provision in the contract stipulating that the Peking government was not to use arms purchased from the Taihei Kumiai Consortium against its Chinese opposition. This clause notwithstanding, the Japanese nevertheless endeavored to circumvent criticism altogether by keeping the arms negotiations a secret.[29]

In spite of such precautions, word of the agreement eventually leaked out. The British, now facing the undivided attention of the German military on the western front and unable to prevent the Japanese *fait accompli*, privately criticized the whole affair. One official in the Foreign Office bitterly commented, "From the secrecy one may conclude that neither Japanese nor Chinese are proud of the transaction."[30] Still another cautioned, "The transaction has been concluded by certain pro-Japanese members of the Cabinet and the Northern Military Party so that the stipulation that the arms will not be used against the South should not be taken seriously, and in any case it is difficult to see how it could be enforced."[31]

Reinsch also commented on the baleful effect that Japanese arms and loans were having on the situation within China. He was increasingly disturbed at Washington's apparent disinclination to counter Japan, and he chided his superiors' lack of foresight. For example, he had suggested that Tuan be removed from Chinese politics by appointing him to a military position in Europe. But the State Department ignored Reinsch's advice and, as a consequence, he was led to report in February 1918 that "it is to be regretted that no way was found for taking General Tuan Ch'i-jui out of politics by giving him a dignified national mission abroad in connection with war action. As it is, General Tuan has again been completely identified with the Northern Militarists, . . . and bitter feeling has been aroused against him in the center and south of China."[32] Reinsch, however, did not limit his censure to his own country. In that same report, he delivered a broader indictment against the "liberal powers" for their lack of "efficient, constructive encouragement and assistance" to China.[33]

Unfortunately for the Western powers, Japan continued to devise methods to extend "efficient, constructive encouragement and assistance" to Tuan. Such aid was increasingly necessary, since popular support for the Peking regime deteriorated as it became more and more identified with Japanese interests. By February 1918, Jordan reported that Tuan's government was "daily losing influence and appears to be practically doomed." He cautioned, however, that with Japanese money and arms, the regime might retain control north of the Yangtze River.[34]

Jordan presently believed that a political resolution to the internal conflict might be at hand, and that either the country would be split into two parts or, more likely, that a coalition regime would be established with the anti-Tuan southern faction receiving a large share in the government. He believed that the reason the South had made such steady progress in the preceding five months was fairly straightforward: "The South, with all its faults, stands for the restoration of Parliamentary Government, and the North stands for nothing but its own interests."[35]

The mounting evidence of the resilience and viability of the southern government indicated that Tuan's northern regime would require still further assistance from Tokyo. The fall of the provisional government in Russia and the consequent fear of the spread of bolshevism presented just such an opportunity to the Japanese. In view of the chaotic and possibly threatening situation in Siberia, General (and later prime minister) Tanaka Giichi, vice-chief of the Japanese general staff, proposed to the Chinese minister in Tokyo the formation of a Sino-Japanese military alliance. The ensuing negotiations culminated in an exchange of notes on 25 March, and the formal signing on 16 and 19 May of the Sino-Japanese Joint Defensive Military Agreement, under which Japanese military forces were allowed to operate from within Chinese territories.[36] Quickly some 16,000 Japanese troops occupied the northeastern provinces of Kirin and Heilungkiang, as well as the route of the Eastern Manchurian Railway, on the pretext of military needs in Siberia. In the words of one historian, these agreements, which provided a legal basis for the presence of a substantial number of Japanese troops within China, were "a remarkable diplomatic achievement for the Terauchi cabinet."[37]

The significance of the Sino-Japanese agreements and their probable impact on Chinese affairs were not lost on Sir John Jordan. In March he warned the Foreign Office that the situation in China was critical; Tuan, who aspired to play a leading role in directing China, had practically admitted the necessity of cooperating with Japan to attain his goal. Therefore Jordan speculated that the military alliance had a political counterpart that would help bolster the position of the North in its struggle against the South.[38]

By the time the agreements were signed in May, Jordan concluded that there was ample evidence that Japan was giving "special support" to Tuan's government. Such interference in Chinese affairs had led to public outcry against the military convention, because Japan was deliberately supporting the military autocracy of the Peking government against the Southerners who, in spite of their faults, fought for a form of constitutional government. Jordan believed that the Japanese pursued such a policy out of the fear that republican ideas would spread from China to Japan: "Representing as Japan does the last stronghold of military theocracy in the Far East, a strong republican China would constitute a perpetual menace to her internal polity."[39]

In spite of this bleak assessment of Sino-Japanese affairs, Jordan was not a complete pessimist. He foresaw that while Japan would dominate China for the duration of the war, the "temporary eclipse of Western influence" would pass away with the return of peace.[40] Indeed, not only would the return of the Western powers to China adversely affect Japan's position, but the Chinese themselves would have a role to play: "If this war has taught us anything, surely one of its principal lessons is that arrangements made with ruling cliques, military or otherwise, have no lasting endurance unless they have the support of the people behind them."[41] However, Jordan's prediction of the future was inaccurate in several respects. While the Chinese themselves eventually did overturn Tuan's clique, they had no desire to see foreigners reimpose the pre-war supremacy they had enjoyed in China; thus, although after the war Japan would fail to dominate China as it had between 1914 and 1918, the Western powers were likewise unable to dominate China as they had before World War I.

Jordan also failed to see that Japan's position in China would come under attack even before the armistice in November. Although Washington had not supported any positive initiatives to deal with the situation in China, Reinsch's hands were not tied, as were Jordan's, by a formal alliance to Japan. Thus Reinsch was free to make proposals for allied actions that were designed to negate those policies by which Japan had extended its influence. The first measure in this regard would be a ban on loans to China in order to deny Tuan access to Japanese funds. Before the end of 1918, the United States also suggested that the powers embargo arms sales to China in order to force the Chinese to end their civil war and negotiate their differences peacefully. Although the arms embargo and the loan ban were presented as altruistic proposals to end the bloodshed and financial waste in China, actually both measures were designed to weaken the pro-Japanese Tuan government in Peking and hasten its fall from power. Thus the Japanese soon discovered that their wartime policies had achieved no lasting results other than arousing the suspicion and hostility of both the Chinese and the West.

NOTES

1. See Madeleine Chi, *China Diplomacy*, p. 138, and Shao, p. 46.

2. John William Young, "The Japanese Military and the Chinese Policy of the Hara Cabinet," (Ph.D. Diss., University of Washington 1971), p. 35.

3. John Van Antwerp MacMurray, ed., *Treaties and Agreements with and Concerning China*, vol. 2 (1912-1919) (New York: 1921), pp. 1382-88.

4. Reinsch to Lansing, 26 February 1917, 893.51/1751, FRUS 1917, p. 125.

5. Reinsch to Lansing, 6 August 1917, 893.51/1793, FRUS 1917, p. 135. Ironically, the Japanese minister had expressed to Reinsch the hope that the United States would join the Consortium, ostensibly because the European partners were temporarily unable to carry their shares. However, Reinsch was of the opinion that the "Japanese attitude may be due partly to [the] desire to prevent independent action of the United States, partly owing to [the] realization that Japan may safely join the United States in a formal maintenance of Chinese unity, [and] independence, considering the existing opportunity for infiltration of Japanese influence through special arrangement with all local and central authorities."

6. Reinsch to Lansing, 11 October 1917, 893.51/1819, FRUS 1917, p. 148. See also 24 September 1917, 893.51/1809, and 2 November 1917, 893.51/1824, FRUS 1917, pp. 142 and 152. Reinsch did not, however, advocate reckless lending to the Chinese: "I beg earnestly to recommend that no funds be freely given to the present Government to dispose of, but that all sums which our Government may be disposed to make available should be, first, charged against definite revenues; second, restricted to definite war purposes and controlled so as to remove them from the possibility of manipulation for the purposes of strengthening the military party against the Republicans and of strengthening Japanese influence as against American and foreign interests." Reinsch to Lansing, 16 September 1917, 893.51/1807, FRUS 1917, p. 141.

7. Shao, p. 49.

8. Takeshi, p. 79.

9. Wheeler to Lansing, 14 June 1917, 893.00/2639, FRUS 1917, p. 69.

10. Lansing to Wheeler, 19 June 1917, 893.00/2645b, FRUS 1917, pp. 73-74. Regarding William Jennings Bryan's diplomacy, Michael H. Hunt remarked that "Bryan was guided through the twenty-one demands crisis by a

devotion to peace that overshadowed the principles of the open door. To the President, to the Chinese, and to the Japanese, he had repeatedly insisted right down to the conclusion of the crisis in May that all sides should show neighborliness and patience. 'As Japan and China must remain neighbors,' he soberly advised Wilson in late March 1915, 'it is of vital importance that they should be neighborly, and a neighborly spirit cannot be expected if Japan demands too much, or if China concedes too little.' Two months after Japan had presented her demands to China, Bryan felt he could safely conclude, 'It is evident that each country is suspicious of the other.' When neighborliness failed, the only alternative Bryan seemed to entertain was to hope that the problem would go away." See Michael H. Hunt, *The Making of a Special Relationship* (New York: 1983), p. 223.

11. Reinsch to Lansing, 25 June 1917, 893.00/2627, FRUS 1917, p. 77. See also Bryan to the Japanese Ambassador, 13 March 1915, 793.94/240, FRUS 1915, p. 108. With respect to the United States, Bryan had said that "the activity of Americans has never been political, but on the contrary has been primarily commercial with no afterthought as to their effect upon the governmental policy of China."

12. Lansing to the Japanese Ambassador, 6 July 1917, 793.94/570, FRUS 17, p. 262.

13. Greene to Balfour, 9 August 1917, F.O. 371/377, 156415, PRO.

14. Spring Rice to Lansing, 3 September 1917, 893.00/2700, FRUS 1917, p. 102.

15. Lansing to the Japanese Ambassador, 6 September 1916, 893.00/2701, FRUS 1917, p. 104. See also Lansing to the British Ambassador, 6 September 1917, 893.00/2700, FRUS 1917, pp. 103-104.

16. Lansing to the Japanese Ambassador, 6 September 1916, 893.00/2701, FRUS 1917, p. 104.

17. Jordan to Balfour, 30 October 1917, F.O. 405/224, 2521, PRO.

18. Reinsch to Lansing, 12 October 1917, 893.00/2736, FRUS 1917, pp. 108-9.

19. Jordan to Balfour, 30 October 1917, F.O. 405/224, 2521, PRO. Jordan, however, indicated that such dependence on Japan did have its costs: "The despatches which I have had the honour to address to you of late will have shown that the Government here has been gradually losing credit in the country, and that one of the main causes of the discredit into which it has fallen has been its alleged subservience to Japan." Jordan to Balfour, 20 November 1917, F.O. 405/224, 2569, PRO.

20. Minutes under Jordan to Balfour, 30 October 1917, F.O. 371/377,

2521, PRO.

21. Jordan to Balfour, 30 October 1917, F.O. 405/224, 2521, PRO.

22. Quoted in Pugach, *Reinsch,* p. 243.

23. For a discussion of the Lansing-Ishii negotiations, see Beers, pp. 34-41.

24. Reinsch to Lansing, 4 November 1917, 793.94/587, FRUS 1917, pp. 265-66.

25. Chinese Minister to the Secretary of State, 12 November 1917, 793.84/603, FRUS 1917, p. 270. Iriye, *Across the Pacific,* p. 136.

26. Daniel James Gage, "Paul S. Reinsch and Sino-American Relations" (Ph.D. diss., Stanford University, 1939), pp. 428-30.

27. Quoted in Scanlan, p. 293.

28. MacMurray, vol. 2, p. 1415.

29. Ibid., p. 1412. In this instance, the Japanese attempted to do so citing military necessity by writing into the agreements the clause: "This agreement and the supplementary articles therein shall not be published by the two Governments, but shall be considered as military secrets."

30. Minutes by LWL under Jordan to Balfour, 26 January 1918, F.O. 371/3177, 61821, PRO.

31. Minute by RM under Greene to Balfour, 15 January 1918, F.O. 371/3177, 9737, PRO.

32. Reinsch to Lansing, 12 February 1918, 893.00/2780, FRUS 1918, p. 84.

33. Ibid., p. 86. Likewise Jordan was not above oblique criticism of the course Britain was forced to pursue because of the war in Europe. At the end of May he reported that "China is in the melting pot and the country is practically being put up for auction, with only one bidder at the sale. . . . As in Yüan's time, we have a military autocracy in Peking, the great difference being that the present one is supported by foreign money and is as inefficient as his was efficient." Jordan to Langley, 29 May 1918, F.O. 350/16, PRO.

34. Jordan to Balfour, 23 February 1918, F.O. 371/3183, 35020, PRO. As was noted in the Foreign Office, Tuan was playing an exceedingly difficult game: "Tuan, who is ambitious of succeeding to the position of Yüan Shih-k'ai, apparently believes he can best do this by falling in with the Japanese; but the Japanese are the least popular foreigners in China, and an open pro-Japanese policy on his part would strengthen his opponents." Minute under Jordan to Balfour, 20 March 1918, F.O. 371/3183, 100061, PRO.

35. Jordan to Langley, 17 February 1918, F.O. 350/16, PRO. The political situation in China was at times difficult to read; just two months later a perplexed Jordan would report: "I have nothing encouraging to say of China

which is still being torn by internal dissentions, so complicated that even I, a fairly old hand at the game, find it hard to unravel the tangled skein." Jordan to Langley, 15 April 1918, F.O. 350/16, PRO.

36. For the texts of these agreements, see MacMurray, 2:1407-15.

37. Shao, p. 50.

38. Jordan to Langley, 6 March 1918, F.O. 350/16, PRO. Jordan to Balfour, 20 March 1918, F.O. 405/224, 10061, PRO. Jordan did not believe that he could predict the outcome of such a situation: "The Government of China as at present constituted, is thoroughly identified with Japan, and the association is one which can hardly fail to have far-reaching consequences, the nature of which it is impossible to forecast at present." Jordan to Balfour, 18 April 1918, F.O. 405/224, 105793, PRO.

39. Jordan to Balfour, 22 May 1918, F.O. 224/224, 128578, PRO. Reinsch also reported on the outcry which the military agreements provoked: "Criticism directed against the agreement dwelt on the absolute secrecy of the negotiations, the exclusion of the other Allies from participating therein, and the possibility that under the agreement far-reaching claims for intervention in Chinese affairs and control of Chinese resources might subsequently be introduced." Reinsch to Lansing, 29 June 1918, 893.00/2868, FRUS 1918, p. 106.

40. Jordan to Langley, 29 May 1918, F.O. 350/16, PRO.

41. Jordan to Langley, 6 March 1918, F.O. 350/16, PRO. Jordan also speculated at this time that "the military cooperation between China and Japan is likely to have far reaching results and may even be the dawn of a coming Pan-Asiatic movement." However, after the Chinese outcry at the signing of the Sino-Japanese military agreements, he reversed his position and could not agree with those who believed in the eventual formation of a Pan-Asiatic movement under the direction of Japan. See Jordan to Langley, 29 May 1918, F.O. 350/16, PRO.

3

The Ban on Loans
to China

Reinsch's dissatisfaction with the situation in China led him to request permission from the State Department to visit the United States. His numerous reports from Peking had failed to produce an infusion of American capital or to increase Washington's influence in China. He hoped, however, that his voice would be more persuasive than his pen in convincing American businessmen and policy makers to play a more active role in Chinese affairs. Although in 1917 Washington twice deemed such a trip to be inappropriate, on 21 June 1918 the State Department finally instructed Reinsch to return to the United States for consultations.[1]

Before turning the legation over to John Van Antwerp MacMurray, Reinsch composed a series of despatches that set the tone for his trip. At the end of June he regretted to report no improvement in the Chinese situation, and in darker moments, even referred to conditions in China as "deplorable."[2] He admitted that although the civilian officials of the central government were generally amenable to a compromise settlement with their southern rivals, they were unable to prevent military leaders from continuing their efforts to resolve the dispute by force of arms. In this regard, Premier Tuan Ch'i-jui was the worst offender, for he argued that

any cessation of military action would be interpreted as weakness which would merely encourage the South to make more extravagant demands and to encroach further upon Northern territory. In his view the question of authority must be settled once for all by imparting to the military movement against the South adequate force. For this purpose money is essential. If domestic revenue is insufficient, foreign loans must be resorted to. The sooner national unity is restored by force, the sooner will it be possible to repay these loans and to establish a system of sovereign control which will reform the army, protect the people and make the country more prosperous.[3]

Since Chinese tax revenues could not cover both the normal operating expenses of the government and the maintenance of a large army in the field against the South, the only alternative "was a willingness, to speak euphemistically, to borrow from the nearest lender at almost any terms."[4]

Reinsch continued to censure Tuan for the policies he pursued, and considered specious the premier's defense of the expedient of resorting to foreign loans. Nevertheless Reinsch continued to believe that Tuan was an honest and even patriotic man, but one who was unfortunately "very strong headed in pursuing a thing once decided upon."[5] He also attempted to absolve Tuan from sole responsibility for China's collapse into quasi-anarchy by blaming in part the military commanders with whom the premier was forced to work.

The situation was not yet hopeless, and Reinsch offered his superiors a simple prescription for China's ills. Since the government had fallen into the hands of corrupt warlords, who exploited the country supported by foreign loans, the "cessation of foreign loans would put an end to military intrigue if it could be made known to the Japanese Government that loan activities are viewed with apprehension as inconsistent with responsibilities, as the temporary representative of Allied interest in China."[6] Reinsch believed that some kind of ban on Japanese loans to the Chinese would have two beneficial results: to check the spread of Japanese influence and to end peaceably China's internal dispute.

Although he had left Peking for Washington with high hopes for positive American aid to China, Reinsch's pleas fell on sympathetic, but ultimately deaf ears. In the course of a month, Reinsch managed to see the representatives of most of the major public and private interests involved in China. Furthermore, he had numerous conferences with Lansing, Undersecretary of State Frank Polk, and even two interviews with President Wilson. But in spite of such efforts, he brought no concrete proposals for American assistance back to China.[7]

Reinsch's failure was largely a product of poor timing. The chief concern of the departments and boards he consulted was to train and transport the U. S. Army to Europe. Compared with this overriding priority, China's participation in the war against Germany, let alone Chinese affairs in general, "shrivelled" in comparison.[8] Reinsch, of course, appreciated the necessity to win the war, but nevertheless he "deeply regretted that a tiny rivulet out of the vast streams of financial strength directed to Europe could not pass to

China." Writing several years after the war, he expressed his belief that "even one thousandth part of the funds given to Europe, invested in building up China, would have prevented many disheartening and disastrous developments."[9] Ironically, even as Reinsch was sailing towards the United States, those very financial interests and government departments destined to disappoint him were nevertheless in the process of initiating a sequence of events that would begin to undermine Japanese influence in China before the end of the year.

On 8 July 1918 a group of American banks (led by J. P. Morgan & Co.) responded favorably to Lansing's request that they consider a loan to China. Before agreeing to proceed further with the negotiations, however, the bankers requested that the American public be informed that such a loan was being made at Washington's suggestion, and that a four-power body, including representatives of Great Britain, France, and Japan, be formed to consider the matter. Basically the bankers believed that through the "cooperation of England, France, Japan and the United States much can be accomplished for the maintenance of Chinese sovereignty and the preservation of the 'open door.'"[10]

Lansing, obviously encouraged by the bankers' note, favored them with a reply the next day in which he addressed each of their concerns: the administration would not hesitate to announce that it had suggested a loan be made, and the formation of a four-power group to deal with China seemed advisable. However, just as significant was Lansing's ringing declaration: "I think that I should say frankly that this Government would be opposed to any terms or conditions of a loan which sought to impair the political control of China or lessened the sovereign rights of the Republic."[11] While ostensibly written to American bankers, this statement was intended for a wider audience. The very next day the Japanese ambassador, as well as his British and French counterparts, received copies of the Lansing-banker exchanges, thus serving notice of the direction of American policy.[12]

Ultimately, however, Lansing and the State Department were to be disappointed in their hopes for the prompt establishment of a new financial organization that would coordinate loans to China. The delay revolved around American plans for this body's scope of operation. The existing Six Power China Consortium had made only "administrative" loans to the Chinese government; "industrial" loans were not regulated. Washington wanted the new organization to have control over all types of loans. Thus the proposed body would effectively tie Tokyo's hands; the independent industrial loans to China by Japan that were not prohibited under the Consortium's rules would be eliminated.[13]

For the moment, however, it was not the Japanese but the British who objected to the American proposal. London explained that Japan had insisted that industrial loans be removed from the scope of operations of the Six Power Consortium in the fall of 1913; since the Japanese position had not changed, it seemed inexpedient to broach the subject for as long as the war lasted. The British position did not daunt the State Department, as it was assumed that London had taken this stance in order to placate its ally. With the end of Britain's wartime dependence on Japan, Washington expected that the British could be coaxed into following America's lead.[14]

Although eventual British support for the control of Japanese loans to China would be significant, even more important was the attitude of Woodrow Wilson. On 14 August Reinsch had composed a memorandum based on his discussions with the president in which he wrote that the "primary and immediate" needs with respect to Chinese political and financial affairs were: "(1) To establish China's public finance on a sound basis [and] (2) The radical suppression of the present debauching practice of making so-called industrial loans the proceeds of which are diverted to corrupt politicians and military machinations." In communicating Reinsch's memorandum to Lansing on 22 August, Wilson commented: "I agreed with him [Reinsch] at the time in the judgments he here expresses." With some satisfaction, Lansing replied to the president two days later that Reinsch's views were in complete accord with those of the department, and were in the process of execution via the formation of an international consortium to make loans to China.[15]

The U.S. show of resolve particularly satisfied Sir John Jordan. In a private letter of 2 August, he noted that the American position on loans to China[16] had created "the latest sensation," and that "it is time that some Power stepped in to stop the criminal folly of the Japanese. The latter had a splendid opportunity of showing a statesmanlike policy in this country during the war, but have thrown it all away in a huckstering spirit unworthy of a great nation. Their record in China during the past four years will recoil upon themselves."[17] Jordan noted that some prescient Japanese, such as Minister Baron Hayashi at Peking, also recognized the harm caused by Tokyo's policies. Hayashi regarded Count Terauchi's personal agents in China "with special horror," even to the point of calling Nishihara the "Japanese Rasputin." Jordan noted that Hayashi particularly resented the irregular methods by which the Terauchi government supported Tuan's regime, and believed that the dual representation Japan maintained in China, that by the official legation and unofficially by Nishihara, "may serve its purpose for a time, but will do no good in the end. Any temporary advantage will be poor compensation for loss of good name."[18]

The emerging U.S. resolve to throttle the flow of yen from Tokyo to Peking marked a watershed in the great power rivalry in China. For four years, Japan had successfully encroached upon China's sovereignty; but from the summer of 1918 onward, with the end of World War I daily more probable, Tokyo was put on the defensive and forced to fend off initiatives intended to dispossess Japan of its wartime gains in order to restore order and stability to the Far East.[19] The crucial question was how the Japanese would respond to this counteroffensive.

Hara Takashi formulated Tokyo's reaction because the Terauchi cabinet fell from power in September 1918. Hara was the first untitled man to hold the office of prime minister; such a change was significant because the Satsuma and Choshu clans, which had alternated power since the Meiji Restoration, had given the military a preeminent voice in government affairs. Hara, as leader of a Seiyukai party which had the support of leading commercial, industrial, and financial groups, was expected to favor these interests, which desired better relations and expanded trade with the United States.[20]

The most serious diplomatic obstacles Hara faced in order to achieve his goal were obviously the China policies of his predecessors, which were manifested physically in Tuan's so-called War Participation Army of three divisions and four mixed brigades. This force was ostensibly created to fight in World War I but never left China. Nonetheless Japanese loans amply bankrolled it, and the possibility that Tuan would use these troops in China's civil war had aroused suspicion in Washington and London. For this very reason, in the months before he became prime minister, Hara opposed the aid-Tuan policy pursued by the Terauchi cabinet. As he confided in his diary in July 1918:

The post-war world will be divided into three blocks centering on the United States, Great Britain, and Germany. The remaining countries will either become satellites of these powers, or will maintain their existence on the basis of the balance of power prevailing among the three titans. Fortunately, Japan is the ally of Britain. If the United States can be brought into this alliance and the cooperation of the three countries established, the future position of Japan will be very secure indeed. On the other hand, if Japan becomes estranged from the United States, the existence of our country will be greatly endangered.[21]

While hoping to cooperate with the West, Hara did not advocate a wholesale Japanese retreat from China. Instead one can agree with Iriye that Hara's government desired to curtail wartime excesses and have Japan act again as a respectable imperial power.[22] Thus Hara believed that future operations in China had to be undertaken in ways designed to minimize foreign suspicions.[23]

Nevertheless Hara faced potentially crippling opposition to his foreign policy. Yamagata Aritomo, the architect of Japan's modern army, was the principal figure in the extra-constitutional group of elder statesmen known as the *Genro*; from this position he wielded considerable power and had earned his reputation as Japan's cabinetmaker and breaker. Yamagata, acting through the autonomous army and navy ministries, was able to defeat both domestic and foreign policies that he did not favor.[24]

Certain provisions within Japan's constitution also worked against Hara. The military were able to circumvent civilian control because the Meiji Constitution was interpreted to give it the exclusive "right of supreme command"; in matters of tactics and operations, the military was not controlled by the cabinet and had the right to report directly to the emperor. This "tendency to act independently of civilian officials had become especially pronounced after the overthrow of the Manchu dynasty in 1912."[25] The service ministries, and especially the Kwantung Army stationed in China, were thus able to formulate and execute their own policies regardless of the position of the civilian government. The assassination of the warlord Chang Tso-lin in 1928 and the Manchurian Incident of 1931 testified to the persistence of this relationship between the Japanese military and civilian government. Hara was therefore in an unenviable position: if he conceded too little to the West in China, he might find himself diplomatically isolated, while if he conceded too much, Yamagata and the military could thwart the policy or even force him from office.

A multitude of problems centering around Chinese affairs therefore confronted Hara from the very outset of his administration. On 8 October Lansing formally presented to the Japanese ambassador in Washington the American proposal to form an international financial body to consider all types of loans to China, which was obviously intended to end independent Japanese activities.[26] In addition, events within China were also working against Japan. The northern government had elected Hsü Shih-ch'ang president in September, an occurrence believed to presage a peaceful reconciliation between the two factions.[27] An optimistic MacMurray advised Washington, "I am strongly of the opinion that now is the psychological and potent time for an expression by President Wilson of the hope that a peaceful and effective adjustment of the dispute between the northern and southern provinces of China be effected and that he stands ready to use his good offices in the premises."[28] He also reported that the foreign and Chinese presses, as well as most of the Chinese with whom the legation was in contact, freely made suggestions that either alone, or in concert with the British or all the Allies, the United States should offer its mediation. Ominously, he warned that every week's delay would make more difficult the application in China of the principle that in the postwar era "strong nations shall not be free to wrong weak nations and make them subject to their purpose and interest" that Wilson had expressed in a speech on 27 September. [29]

Wilson acted quickly on MacMurray's advice. On 10 October, without consulting either Tokyo or London, Wilson telegraphed Hsü, offering congratulations on his accession to the presidency. Wilson's message contained political overtones, for in it he declared that the time had arrived for the leaders of China to put aside their differences in order to unify the country. Significantly, Wilson deemed unification to be the top priority because "China is torn by internal dissentions so grave that she must compose these before she can fulfil [*sic*] her desire to cooperate with her sister nations [in the European war]."[30] The Japanese could easily construe this statement as a diplomatic snub since Tuan was ostensibly training the War Participation Army for service in World War I with Japan's guidance. The Japanese apparently suffered yet another blow when Tuan resigned the premiership in the wake of Wilson's message.[31]

All seemed to augur well for China's future, but such was not the case. Although it was true that Tuan no longer retained his civilian office, his power remained largely intact as head of the War Participation Bureau. Jordan commented that in this capacity, Tuan was undoubtedly very useful to Japan and still presented a formidable obstacle to any political settlement between the North and South.[32] Furthermore, in spite of the newly cooperative attitude of the Japanese government, Tokyo was reluctant to follow American initiatives. For example, a full week after Wilson's telegram to Hsü, the Japanese minister for foreign affairs, Uchida Yasuya, told the British ambassador that he had not yet seen a copy of the president's message, and lamely suggested that such declarations were counterproductive since they could offend the South. As was noted within the Foreign Office, the real reason for this sour attitude was the distaste the Japanese had for any independent action by foreign governments in Chinese affairs.[33]

In contrast, Jordan was elated at the course of events: "Now that the United States is beginning to take an active interest in the affairs of the Far East one may hope that some form of international co-operation will be evolved, which will save China from the aggressive encroachments of Japan and the predatory instincts of her own pseudo militarism."[34] By the end of October 1918 Reinsch reported that the Japanese had finally "read the spirit of the times" and had concluded that "the backing of the Chinese military clique in prolonging civil strife has served its purpose and that a different policy must now be inaugurated."[35] In this regard, on 24 October 1918 the Japanese at last consented to the sending of a joint note to the leaders of the North and South advocating the restoration of peace. A Foreign Office official minuted smugly that "this is satisfactory and shows that the representations which we made recently to the Japanese . . . have not been without effect."[36]

Unfortunately such self-satisfaction was premature. The powers had, after all, only approved that a pious, and toothless, declaration be made to both sides. On a more forceful level, the British had, since September, suggested that the powers apply fiscal pressure on the Chinese in order to expedite the peace process.[37] But just two days after cooperating with the West by approving the joint note to the warring factions, the Hara government refused the request to stop the flow of money to China because "any such procedure might hurt the pride of the Chinese, and might, in the end, do more harm than good."[38]

Jordan was wholly unimpressed by the Japanese argument, writing that the "question of Chinese pride is not so important as [the] *interests of our own people* (emphasis added) and of those of law and order in this country and [the] withholding of funds is [the] only means we can use for putting stop to [the] criminal folly of armed conflicts between North and South."[39] Although he added that it was "a moral obligation which strongly influenced" the British position, Jordan's statement starkly exposed the priorities upon which he based his recommendations.[40]

Ultimately, however, the Hara government, faced with continuous Western prodding, and with the end of the European war a reality, relented, and instructed Japanese banks to suspend advances on loans to the Chinese government. Jordan noted on 11 November 1918 that this announcement by

Tokyo had "alarmed Military authorities [in China] as they are almost entirely dependent on this money for support of their troops. . . . Funds in hand will suffice to meet Military expenditures for the next six months."[41] With this move to restrict the funds flowing to China, the Western powers had taken the first step towards weakening Japan's position in that country. The logical corollary to this economic offensive was an arms embargo to curtail further the power of the pro-Japanese faction in Chinese affairs.

NOTES

1. Pugach, *Reinsch,* p. 250.
2. Reinsch to Lansing, 26 June 1918, 893.51/1913 and 27 June 1918, 893.00/2866, DSNA.
3. Reinsch to Lansing, 29 June 1918, 893.00/2868, FRUS 1918, p. 102.
4. Ibid. These particular remarks were not printed in FRUS 1918, so the DSNA files should be consulted. To emphasize his point, Reinsch offered the following commentary: "The financial destitution of the Central Government . . . led the officials of the Central Government, as well as of many provinces, to take recourse to foreign loans. During the quarter among the more important loans, *all Japanese* [emphasis added], there were a loan of twenty million yen, secured on the revenues of the Government telegraph system, . . . a loan of twenty million yen for additional construction on the Kirin-Changchun Railway; a loan of three million yen to Fengtien Province for the redemption of small coin notes, secured on collieries; a number of other loans were in the process of negotiation, secured on mining rights and Government revenues. The larger part of the proceeds of these loans, for whatever purpose avowedly constructed, *were used to defray military operations* [emphasis added]. . . . The wholesale pledging of important national revenues and resources for such a purpose was bitterly condemned and resented by the Chinese people. The bearing of the liens and concessions granted in these loan contracts on the commercial rights and opportunities of other nations remains to be seen." See FRUS 1918, pp. 107-108.
5. Reinsch to Lansing, 27 June 1918, 893.00/2866, DSNA.
6. Reinsch to Lansing, 26 June 1918, 893.51/1913, DSNA.
7. Paul Reinsch, *An American Diplomat in China* (Garden City, N.Y.: 1922), pp. 354-55. Pugach, *Reinsch,* pp. 251-52.

8. Reinsch, p. 356.

9. Ibid., pp. 356-57.

10. Certain American Bankers to the Secretary of State, 8 July 1918, 893.51/2176, FRUS 1918, p. 173.

11. Lansing to Certain American Bankers, 9 July 1918, 893.51/2176, FRUS 1918, p. 174.

12. See note 1 under Lansing to Reading, 10 July 1918, 893.51/1923c, FRUS 1918, p. 175.

13. Beers, pp. 144-46. Some revisionist historians have overlooked the importance of the attempt to ban independent industrial loans to China in their assessments of U.S. policy. For example, on page 54 of her book, *Bankers and Diplomats in China*, Roberta Dayer stated that "in establishing a new Consortium, the United States was joining the other foreign powers in providing financial support for a corrupt and unpopular administration in Peking." In her analysis, however, Dayer overlooked Reinsch's and MacMurray's repeated warnings that any loan to China had to be closely scrutinized to ensure that it would be used constructively and not squandered. The United States did not join the Consortium to support Tuan's regime, but rather attempted to make sure that Japan did not do so.

14. The acting Secretary of State Frank Polk telegraphed to Chargé MacMurray, "The Japanese here in discussing the proposal show an unwillingness to have industrial loans included and are evidently trying also to influence Great Britain and China to declare against their inclusion." Polk to MacMurray, 10 August 1918, 893.51/1951, FRUS 1918, p. 188. Indicative of the mood of the State Department at this juncture is that in a draft of the message, Polk had initially made reference to the fact that "the aim of this Government is to devise plans to end the *evil* [emphasis added] practice" by the Japanese of making loans to China, but that the word "evil" was stricken from the final draft. See also Beers, pp. 145-46.

15. See the correspondence of 14, 22, and 24 August 1918 in 893.51/1979, DSNA. Chargé MacMurray's views were also essentially in accord with the State Department. On 6 August 1918, in a telegram only partly recorded on pages 186-87 of FRUS 1918, he advised, "It should be, if possible, arranged with the governments concerned that both political and industrial loans to the Central Government or to the provinces should all be made through the consortium." Furthermore his assessment of Chinese affairs was similar to Reinsch's: "All authority centers in Premier Tuan who commands no support in the country save in so far as he is able by periodical money payments to

retain the backing of certain military leaders. . . . All money that now comes into the hands of this government is therefore squandered upon the perpetuation of a futile civil war carried on in the interest of a small self-seeking clique of military politicians." MacMurray to Polk, 6 August 1918, 893.51/1951, DSNA.

16. See Polk to Page, 30 July 1918, 893.51/1945a, FRUS 1918, pp. 181-82.

17. Jordan to Macleay, 2 August 1918, F.O. 350/16, PRO.

18. See Jordan to Macleay, 2 and 14 August, and Jordan to Langley, 28 August 1918, F.O. 350/16, PRO.

19. Akira Iriye, *After Imperialism* (Cambridge: 1965), pp. 13-14.

20. Beers, p. 139.

21. Quoted in John Young, p. 37.

22. Iriye, *After Imperialism*, p. 9.

23. John Young, p. 41.

24. Ibid., p. 14.

25. Iriye, *After Imperialism*, pp. 8-9. For example, beginning in August 1918, Japan's Siberian policy was controlled by the military, and troop movements were undertaken without consultation with civilian officials. Ambassador Morris telegraphed from Tokyo in early September that "recent events seem to support the statement constantly repeated that the General Staff has a definite policy in Siberia and that it proposes to pursue this policy leaving to the Foreign Office and Viscount Ishii the task of explaining after the event." Morris to Polk, 8 September 1918, 861.77/466, FRUS 1918 (Russia, vol. 3), p. 245.

26. See Lansing to Morris, 8 October 1918, 893.51/2038a, FRUS 1918, pp. 196-97.

27. MacMurray to Lansing, 17 September 1918, 893.00/2877, FRUS 1918, p. 110.

28. MacMurray to Lansing, 4 October 1918, 893.00/2882, DSNA.

29. Ibid. See also MacMurray to Lansing, 8 October 1918, 893.00/2906, DSNA.

30. President Woodrow Wilson to President Hsü Shih-ch'ang, 10 October 1918, 893.00/1H85/4, FRUS 1918, p. 111. Wilson's message had a positive impact within China, for at the end of October Reinsch reported that "the reference to reconstituting national unity in the President's telegram to President Hsü has made a profound impression, it has been welcomed by leaders and the public as counsel inspired by true friendship. The press is filled with reports that the American and British ministers were working for

peace." Reinsch to Lansing, 26 October 1918, 893.00/2896, DSNA.

31. As the result of a political compromise between the various factions comprising the northern regime, Tuan had stated that he would resign when Feng Kuo-chang's term as acting president expired in September. See MacMurray to Lansing, 17 September 1918, 893.00/2877, FRUS 1918, p. 110, and Madeleine Chi, *China Diplomacy*, p. 140.

32. Jordan to Balfour, 15 October 1918, F.O. 371/3184, 173031, PRO.

33. Minute under Greene to Balfour, 17 October 1918, F.O. 371/3184, 174390, PRO.

34. Jordan to Balfour, 23 October 1918, F.O. 405/224, 205337, PRO. Furthermore, with respect to great power cooperation in China, Jordan offered his superiors the opinion "that Great Britain and America could formulate and carry out a policy for the reform of China I have very little doubt, but whether they could do it in concert with Japan and France I am by no means so certain."

35. Reinsch to Lansing, 26 October 1918, 893.00/2896, DSNA.

36. Minute under Greene to Balfour, 24 October 1918, F.O. 371/3184, 178284, PRO. The European armistice interrupted the discussions pertaining to the wording of the joint representation, so it was not presented until 2 December 1918.

37. Balfour to Jordan, 14 September 1918, F.O. 371/3184, 155149, PRO.

38. Balfour to Greene, 26 October 1918, F.O. 405/224, 180484, PRO.

39. Jordan to Balfour, 31 October 1918, F.O. 371/3184, 181293, PRO.

40. Shortly after the war, the Department of Overseas Trade communicated to the Foreign Office its concerns about the promotion of British interests and the stability of China: "[The Foreign Office's communications pertaining to Japan's loans to China] emphasize the seriousness of the present situation and the detrimental effects on the future of British trade and enterprise in China which are bound to result from the continuance of the policy which Japan is now pursuing. . . . China is one of the three great areas of future expansion, and the promotion of British enterprise and trade in those areas, desirable as it was before the war, will after the war be a matter of immediate and vital necessity. But development in China after the war requires as the preliminary condition the cessation of the internal struggle which is at present disturbing the country. It is moreover clear that Japan, as security for the advances she has made, has obtained control over coal mines, mineral resources, forests, railways, and telegraphs and other valuable concessions in China. From past experience it

may be supposed that any advantage which Japan derives from such control will be used primarily, if not exclusively, in her own interests, and the resulting situation will constitute a real menace to our free commercial development." Department of Overseas Trade to the Foreign Office, 25 November 1918, F.O. 371/3190, 195549, PRO.

41. Jordan to Balfour, 11 November 1918, F.O. 371/3184, 187343, PRO. R.M. minuted, "The attitude taken by the Japanese government is satisfactory and the stoppage of these loan advances should have a good effect on the Northern Military Party."

4

The China Arms Embargo

The armistice that ended World War I had worldwide repercussions. In the Far East not only did the termination of hostilities presage a resurgence of Western influence, but Tokyo found itself handicapped because it could no longer loan money to Peking under the pretense that the funds would be used to prepare Chinese troops to fight in France. The same was true regarding the sale of Japanese arms to China. Central to Japan's wartime arms sales were two loans, one of 18,716,421 yen concluded on 30 December 1917 and the other of 13,365,126 yen on 31 July 1918 that the Taihei Kumiai Consortium made to Peking, enabling China to purchase Japanese equipment. These funds were used to equip the War Participation Army that Tuan's War Participation Bureau administered.

Even as the Western powers moved to curtail Japan's unilateral loans to China in the fall of 1918, Minister Reinsch focused the State Department's attention squarely on the War Participation Bureau and Army, describing them as the physical manifestations of Japan's machinations. In a telegram of 19 October that is worthy of extended quotation, Reinsch portrayed the situation in Manichean terms:

Political affairs in Peking have reached a stage of deep degradation. Sinister factors . . . have further developed.

The Military clique are attempting to make the War Participation Bureau the center of their influence on the Government. General Tuan is now at its head. It is given control of business relating to finance, natural resources, and police over the heads of the powerless ministries. It uses Japanese financial support and debauches Government finances by corrupt expenditures on a vast scale. . . . In all respects, the methods of this clique are insolent and ruthless including an absolute suspension of all free discussion in the newspapers which are terrorized through frequent police interference. . . . This organization is attempting to fix upon the country military rule under Tuan. While supposedly devoted to prepare for participation in [the] European war, [the] only aim [of the] War Participation Bureau appears to be personal enrichment of [this] clique and their control of [the] country through corrupt and ruthless means. . . . This organization involves a denial of every principle of national and international action for which [the] Allies are fighting. . . . The country from end to end is suffering under their abuses but organized opposition is prevented by [a] sinister outside influence which works with corrupt elements wheresoever found and paralyze sound action.[1]

Ominously, Reinsch warned that "if this attempt of Japanese military absolutism to control China through its military is successful, the issues of the present war will have to be fought over again within a generation."[2] The State Department did not, however, favor the Peking Legation with an immediate reply, probably owing to the complexities of Asian affairs, as well as the pressing need to conclude the armistice in Europe.

Washington's initial response to the problems posed by the War Participation Army came in early December 1918, in the form of a reply to a telegram sent by Chargé d'Affaires MacMurray on 8 October. At that time, MacMurray had brought to the department's attention the fact that an American firm wanted an export license to ship arms and ammunition to Hunan province. Although the local Chinese officials had indicated that they intended to use the arms to suppress brigandage, MacMurray pointed out that since the civil war was being fought in and around the province, the department should carefully review the request, and not grant the necessary permits as a matter of routine.[3]

Acting Secretary of State Polk replied two months later, requesting on 6 December further recommendations concerning the situation in Hunan. But ultimately much more significant was Polk's statement, undoubtedly influenced by Reinsch's telegram of 19 October, that "you may at your discretion discuss with your colleagues the restriction of supplies of arms and ammunition as well as of funds in connection with the plans for reconciliation of north and south."[4] Thus Washington perceived that both a loan ban and an arms embargo would be necessary corrective measures to weaken Tuan's War Participation Army, and by extension, Japanese influence in China.

Reinsch, now of the opinion that "the radical suppression of the military nuisance is the basic of all reform in China," quickly set about organizing the arms embargo.[5] Toward this end, Reinsch for a change enjoyed some quick success. On 9 December Jordan requested authority from London to join in a declaration by the powers that no arms or ammunition be sold to either side pending a settlement of their differences.[6] Less than a week later, Paris indicated its willingness to participate in such a statement. In informing London of the French decision, and undoubtedly in an attempt to expedite similar action by the Foreign Office, Jordan opined, "Personally I do not see how any Government who desires peace in China can object to it."[7] Jordan received the requisite authorization from London four days later.

The Japanese, however, had no desire to follow the American lead. An example of the disparity between the Japanese rhetoric favoring cooperation with the West and the reluctance to make this policy a reality took place on 25 December 1918. That day Hara addressed the Japanese Diet declaring that "the new government renounces the pro-Tuan Ch'i-jui policy of the former cabinet and takes an impartial stand toward North and South. There is no change in Japan's hope of early settlement of Chinese internal differences. To that end, the Japanese Government will cooperate with Britain, the United States, and other Powers concerned."[8] That same day, however, Japanese Vice Minister for Foreign Affairs Shidehara Kijuro told Great Britain's Ambassador Greene that Tokyo could not take any action regarding the proposed joint arms declaration. He explained that the Taihei Kumiai's contract obliged the consortium to make monthly deliveries of arms and ammunition to the Chinese government; for the moment, the Japanese would go no further than to state that they were examining the possibility of postponing deliveries while the Chinese peace negotiations took place.[9]

Two weeks later Japan's minister to Peking, Obata Yukichi, presented Reinsch with a more blunt refusal to cooperate with the West by terminating support to Tuan. Obata declared that, with respect to a twenty million yen loan contract between Japanese banks and the War Participation Bureau, "The Japanese Government was powerless to interfere to prevent its execution." He used the same explanation to disappoint Reinsch's hopes for a prompt arms embargo, saying that it was impossible for the Japanese government to interfere with the Taihei Kumiai shipments "because loss might thus be occasioned to the Company through non-execution of its contract." Therefore Obata argued that Tokyo had no choice but to allow the arms shipments be made until the contract was fulfilled in April 1919. Reinsch attempted to persuade the minister to adopt a different posture and, in his own estimation, he discussed the matter "frankly and fully" with Obata. The Japanese minister, however, would not yield, and only reiterated the view that there was no alternative but to permit the execution of the existing contracts.[10]

Given the persistent criticism from the West, the Japanese tried to develop a convincing justification for the continued existence of Tuan's War Participation Army. On 20 January 1919 Minister Obata told Jordan that in order to disband the armies controlled by the various provincial military governors, Tuan's three divisions would require Japanese equipment. While it was true that the troops controlled by the provincial warlords posed a recognized threat to the peace, and that ways to disband them had been discussed for several months,[11] Jordan nevertheless summarily dismissed Obata's argument:

I said that from my point of view it was a grave mistake to furnish arms to any party in China at the present moment. I placed no faith in Tuan Ch'i-jui's professions [that such arms would not be used against the South] and considered him the main obstacle in the way of peace between the North and South. He was merely organizing a new army for his own aggrandizement and when he had his three Divisions completed, somebody else would in turn start another force to disband his. So long as this sort of thing went on, it was hopeless to expect peace in China.[12]

Such direct language was indicative of the mounting exasperation towards Japanese policy felt within the British Legation.

Given Tokyo's steadfast diplomatic position, Tuan's War Participation Bureau (renamed after the end of World War I the Frontier Defense Bureau, overseeing the Northwest Frontier Defense Army) continued to recruit new troops as well as receive Japanese money and arms. By early February 1919 Obata, who still sought to devise a formula that would make this growing force acceptable to the West, suggested that the powers request from Tuan a pledge that his army would not be used to coerce the South. The Foreign Office and Jordan considered this suggestion "both futile and disingenuous" and speculated that "the Japanese appear still to be secretly working with Tuan Ch'i-jui and the Military Party in the North, thus frustrating all hope of reconciliation with the South."[13]

The Japanese decision to oppose an arms embargo not only increased suspicions about Hara's desire to cooperate with Great Britain; and the United States, but also served to drive Reinsch and Jordan into an ever-closer working relationship.[14] An excellent example of this took place at a 7 February 1919 meeting of the ministers whose countries were interested in the Consortium. Before this forum, Reinsch and Jordan, using language not frequently heard at such gatherings, took the opportunity to castigate Japan for supporting Tuan's army. As Jordan reported to London, Reinsch assumed the initiative and took occasion to dilate upon the highly dangerous situation created by the organization of this force, and declared himself undeceived by the specious protests which were being put forward for its existence. He considered it the duty of the Allied representatives to let the Chinese Government know that they fully appreciated the difficulties to which the President and his party were exposed by the machinations of the military leaders in the North. . . . [Obata] asked what evidence existed that the new divisions were to be used for the purpose of coercing the South. He suggested that the Allied Ministers should join him in a declaration that they would not be so used. I said that the mere fact that such a large force was being raised by the North at a time when both parties were endeavoring to settle their differences by a conference at Shanghai, was quite sufficient evidence that it was not intended for any good purpose and no declaration could have any effect in allaying the apprehensions so generally and justly felt throughout the country.

After these attacks Obata conceded only that he would consult Tokyo on the matter. Jordan, his suspicions fully aroused, prefaced his summary of this diplomatic exchange with an apocalyptic commentary on Japan's policies. He feared that the Japanese wanted to convert China "into a military autocracy in order to perpetuate in Asia the evil system which has just been triumphantly overthrown in Europe." Furthermore, he believed that, with Obata's support, the warlords of Japan and China were pursuing a common policy that "involves nothing less than the military domination of the East by Japan."[15]

Less than a week later, the West's diplomatic pressure on Tokyo increased further. On 12 February the French minister joined Reinsch and Jordan in declaring that the Defense Bureau's continued recruitment of troops constituted a "disturbing element" of the Chinese situation, and that the supplying of money for this purpose was "not desirable."[16] By the end of the month, Paris authorized its minister to warn Tuan against resuming the civil war, which "would produce a deplorable effect among the friendly nations."[17]

Assailed on all sides, Tokyo finally gave ground in order to avoid further estrangement from the other powers. But even in retreat, the Japanese sought to shore up their diplomatic position by assuming a tone of injured innocence; Shidehara, in announcing on 17 February the decision to suspend arms shipments to Tuan, asked Ambassador Greene if it was likely that the Japanese government would support a national army in China to be used to coerce the South at the same time that Tokyo favored a reconciliation between the two parties. Although the Japanese indicated that they would end shipments of arms to Tuan's forces, they would go no further; Greene was informed that payments to China from the War Participation Loan had to be continued since the money had been deposited in private Japanese banks, and a suspension would constitute the first act of bankruptcy.[18]

Would Washington and London be satisfied with the Japanese concession? Tokyo had, after all, apparently agreed to some form of arms embargo for China, although significantly Japan's minister to Peking was not yet authorized to join in a formal declaration to that effect. Having come this far, the Foreign Office saw no need to ease the pressure and instructed Jordan to go even further: "You should, if you consider that such action may strengthen the hands of the President in dealing with Tuan Ch'i-jui and his generals, make representations to him in concert with your Allied colleagues in favor of the disbandment of the new National Defense forces."[19] While formally directed at Tuan, such a request obviously was pointed at Tokyo; if honored, it would have dealt a death blow to Japan's wartime gains in China, because Tuan could not expect to retain influence without his armed forces.[20] Jordan was in complete accord with his instructions from London, believing that the "overthrow of the entire system is a condition precedent to [the] establishment of [an] ordered Government in China."[21]

Unfortunately this kind of rapid change in the Chinese situation was not to be had. With every step away from his predecessor's aid-Tuan policy, Hara had encountered increasing criticism, especially from important elements of the Japanese military. Shidehara gave Chargé MacMurray, recently transferred to Tokyo from Peking, an indication of the pressures the government faced by remarking that "the Cabinet has gone as far as is politically possible in restraining the Japanese military party from its support of the Tuan faction in China."[22] Shidehara's obvious implication was that further concessions might topple the government.

Not only did the Hara government suggest that it had made as many concessions as possible, but it now chose to mount a diplomatic counterattack, perhaps in an effort to restore its credibility with the Japanese military. On 3 March 1919 Obata gave Jordan a memorandum which argued that the British suggestion that the powers press Tuan for the disbandment of his army did not seem to be "wholly reconcilable" with a joint aide-mémoire of 2 December 1918, in which the powers had disclaimed any "desire to control or influence the particular terms of [the peace] adjustment which must remain for the Chinese themselves to arrange."[23] The Japanese note piously declared that in spite of the good intentions of the British government, a disbandment declaration would no doubt be construed as an effort to influence the Shanghai Peace Conference (February-June 1919) between the North and South, and that the Japanese government believed it unwise to act in such a manner.

The disingenuousness of the Japanese argument was readily apparent.[24] With the December note, the powers had attempted to ensure that the Chinese would be allowed to settle their affairs without foreign interference. With the note of 3 March, the Japanese argued that the letter, not spirit, of the December note should be adhered to, in order to maintain Tuan's army and with it the current pro-Japanese balance of power within China.

Japan's attitude had an adverse impact on the Shanghai negotiations. No doubt bolstered by Tokyo's continuing support, Tuan refused the call of the southern delegates to disband the Frontier Defense Army. As a result the peace talks collapsed and the civil war resumed in June 1919.[25] As Reinsch reported, Tuan and his supporters were not alarmed at the prospect of renewed hostilities:

> The feeling is very strong among the representatives at Shanghai, as well as throughout the country, that the Japanese military organization is in no sense abating its support of the Northern militarists. The Hara cabinet has indeed announced that it would discontinue the furnishing of arms and ammunition. But it is well known that the ammunition is already furnished and is in the hands of the Northern militarists, particularly those connected with the War Participation Bureau, which is sufficient to give them an enormous advantage should hostilities be renewed.[26]

Furthermore he reported the concurrent belief that the Japanese military had encouraged Tuan's intransigence, and planned to prolong the Shanghai deliberations in order to buy time "to build up a strong military force in North China, dependent upon Japan[,] with which to defeat any policy of the conference that may be hostile to the maintenance of military ascendancy in China."[27]

The Japanese diplomatic counteroffensive continued on 4 March when Jordan again invited Obata to join in representations in favor of disbandment of the War Participation Army; the Japanese minister countered with an alternative declaration to the effect that the plan of organization of those troops should not be allowed to hamper the Shanghai negotiations. Reinsch and the French minister joined Jordan in rejecting this proposition as worthless.[28]

By the middle of March, Tokyo's arguments defending its policies in China again came under fire. Reinsch remarked that the Japanese suggestion that statements concerning the War Participation Bureau should be avoided, since they could be considered as undue interference with Chinese internal affairs, was not convincing:

Other Ministers believe that as the War Participation Bureau was made the vehicle of negotiations with one of the Allies concerning War activities[,] all [the] Allies are to a certain extent responsible before the Chinese people and the world for action taken by the Bureau while still supposedly enjoying Allied countenance. The withdrawal of countenance is what is proposed. Statements with regard to it can therefore not be considered internal interference.[29]

But an even more difficult question was posed directly to Minister Obata. One of Tokyo's principal defenses of the loan to prepare Chinese forces for World War I was that the contract was a purely commercial affair, over which the Japanese government had no control; Obata was now asked how it was that in connection with this loan Japanese military officers were assigned as instructors and advisers to the bureau, and whether such was the usual Japanese practice for a purely commercial transaction. The apparently flustered Obata could only reply that he was not fully informed on the matter and would have to refer to the documents pertaining to the deal. Reinsch said of Obata's performance that "his disingenuous attitude was plainly disgusting to the other representatives present. One of them remarked to me that it was difficult to remain tolerant of these transparent shams."[30] Ultimately the stimulus that would finally lead the Japanese to alter their policy came from an unexpected quarter.

In the spring of 1919 the Canadian Postal Service had intercepted letters which indicated that three American firms in China, Anderson Meyer and Company, Frazar and Company, and the Barkley Company, were placing orders in the United States, in some cases on behalf of Chinese military governors, for arms and ammunition. The Foreign Office did not believe that the U.S. government had encouraged this trade, yet it could set a dangerous precedent that might lead to a wholesale dumping of arms in China by firms seeking "their share of the profits."[31] Given the delicacy of the situation, Foreign Secretary Arthur Balfour instructed Jordan to broach the subject with Reinsch as tactfully as possible, in such a way as not to reveal the source of the British information.

Jordan found his opportunity to do so at the end of March. At that time, Reinsch freely admitted that he had knowledge of one American firm that sought to sell arms to China, and he said that he had done what he could to discourage the transaction. However, he could do no more since he was not in a position to enforce any prohibition.[32]

This conversation with Jordan could only have disconcerted Reinsch. After having taken such a strong stand against the importation of Japanese arms to China, the fact that he did not have the power to prevent such a trade from the United States must have been particularly galling. But at this moment of acute embarrassment and disappointment, the Japanese unexpectedly changed their position.

The origins of this reversal stemmed from the fact that Japanese intelligence had also come upon evidence of American arms sales to China, and Obata presented Reinsch with accurate figures of the Anderson Meyer deal on 2 April. In stark contrast, however, to the delicate way that Jordan had presented the British findings, Obata jumped at the opportunity to imply that the United States was guilty of duplicity: "The [Anderson Meyer] information appears to me highly incredible in itself in the present circumstances, and moreover, in view of the spirit in which you proposed . . . on December 9th last year to make a joint communication [prohibiting the export of arms to China]."[33] Reinsch retorted that the powers had not yet formally announced the existence of a prohibition on arms sales to China and reminded Obata that it had been the Japanese who the previous December had prevented the formation of an embargo by declining to join in such an agreement. Given that a vast amount of Japanese weaponry had entered the country since that time, Reinsch professed not to understand Japan's concern over what he termed "a small commercial shipment." Reinsch, however, did not content himself merely with exposing the inconsistency in Japan's arguments; instead he turned Obata's newly found interest in arms control to advantage and asked if Tokyo was now willing to accept the embargo.[34] Reinsch could have only been pleasantly surprised when Obata informed him on 4 April that the Japanese government believed the time opportune to agree upon a mutual restriction of the arms trade to China.[35]

What accounted for Tokyo's sudden change of heart? Undoubtedly Reinsch's response to Obata's inquiry into the Anderson Meyer transaction was decisive. Reinsch neither apologized nor pled that he had no power to interfere with it, as he had to Jordan. Rather, Reinsch left Obata with the impression that the Anderson Meyer contract would be the first of many.

Diplomatically, evidence of the ability of the United States to send arms to China was significant; since Reinsch had first proposed the embargo in December 1918, one of the Japanese objections to it had been that, as Japan was the only power able to supply China with arms, the embargo would appear to be directed solely at Tokyo. Although the embargo was indeed intended to restrain Japan, this could not be openly acknowledged, and Reinsch had attempted to argue that many countries were in a position to sell arms to China. With the Anderson Meyer contract, American firms served notice that they were in fact ready and willing to sell arms to the Chinese, which nullified the Japanese objection.

But ultimately more important than diplomatic posturing was the fact that Tokyo now had to face two disagreeable options regarding the situation in China. On the one hand, it could maintain its current policy and continue to ship arms to China under the Taihei contract. However, as the Anderson Meyer negotiations had indicated, to do so meant that Western firms would probably supply the southern faction with arms and ammunition, which would strengthen Tuan's opponents. On the other hand, the Japanese could accept the West's proposed arms embargo. Such a move did entail risk, as it could weaken the Tuan regime in the long run. Given, however, previous Japanese support for Tuan, including the July 1918 Taihei contract, which by March of 1919 was over one-half complete, the North did have a military edge and at least a short-term advantage over the South. Faced with two undesirable alternatives, Tokyo chose what must have appeared to be the lesser of two evils. Thus by early April 1919, both the West and Japan could perceive that the arms embargo was advantageous; for the West it portended the strangulation and eventual fall of the northern military government, while for Japan it represented a freeze in the current status quo, which would maintain the North's military superiority for presumably as long as the embargo was effective.

With the United States, Great Britain and Japan each finally in agreement on the necessity of a China arms embargo, the diplomatic negotiations required to put the agreement together were swiftly completed. On 5 May 1919 Jordan, in his capacity as the dean of the diplomatic corps in China, delivered a note to the acting Chinese minister of foreign affairs, which read in part:

The Governments of Great Britain, Spain, Portugal, the United States, Russia, Brazil, France and Japan have agreed effectively to restrain their subjects and citizens from exporting to or importing into China arms and munitions of war and material destined exclusively for their manufacture until the establishment of a government whose authority is recognized throughout the whole country and also to prohibit during the above period the delivery of arms and munitions for which contracts have already been made but not executed.[36]

Although some imperfections in the agreement would become evident only later, one immediate problem was that China was not a signatory. Although the Chinese were asked to refrain from procuring arms and ammunition for military purposes, no representative of any Chinese faction would agree to the embargo.[37] Thus the Chinese demand for weaponry remained a constant, if not increasing, temptation to those individuals or countries willing to risk criminal prosecution or international disfavor by shipping such material to China. Nevertheless, as a result of the arms embargo and loan ban to China, Reinsch and Jordan could believe that the days of Japanese predominance in China were numbered.

NOTES

1. Reinsch to Lansing, 19 October 1918, 893.00/2893, DSNA. Extracts from this telegram may also be found in FRUS 1918, pp. 112-14.

2. Ibid. MacMurray agreed with Reinsch's estimation of Chinese affairs. In a private letter of 22 October 1918 to Ransford S. Miller, the chief of the Division of Far Eastern Affairs, MacMurray wrote: "The utter degradation of Government by the ruling clique has given occasion for a good many worries, and day and night, all summer, there have been Chinese friends and foreigners coming in to tell what they know of the latest secret deal, so that it has been hard to keep one's head screwed on, and even harder to find an opportunity to get down on paper such grains as might be winnowed out from the chaff." MacMurray Papers, box 58.

3. MacMurray to Lansing, 8 October 1918, 693.119/254, and Reinsch to Lansing, 23 October 1918, 693.119/251, DSNA.

4. Polk to Reinsch, 6 December 1918, 693.119/254, FRUS 1919, p. 667.

5. Reinsch to Lansing, 10 December 1918, 893.51/2079, DSNA. In this telegram, Reinsch also made it clear that it was up to the United States to take the initiative in Chinese affairs. With specific reference to Chinese finances, but applicable to the situation in China as a whole, he advised that "Great Britain, on account of the Japanese Alliance, cannot take the lead, but the British hope for American leadership."

6. Jordan to Balfour, 9 December 1918, F.O. 371/3184, 203168, PRO.

7. Jordan to Balfour, 15 December 1918, F.O. 371/3184, 206816, PRO.

8. Quoted in Takeshi, p. 228.

9. Greene to Balfour, 25 December 1918, F.O. 371/3184, 211693, PRO. Greene had warned London of possible Japanese resistance to an arms

embargo as early as 13 December. See Greene to Balfour, 13 December 1918, F.O. 371/3184, 206158, PRO.

10. Reinsch to Lansing, 10 January 1919, 893.51/2125, FRUS 1919, pp. 291-93. Jordan relayed a similar explanation to London in a message to Balfour, 21 January 1919, F.O. 371/3682, 12566, PRO. The Japanese argument was, however, disingenuous. As John Young noted on page 47, "The Japanese government relieved the arms supplier from any risk by buying the bonds issued by China to secure her debt. This method also had the merit of preserving the appearance of a transaction between China and a private Japanese firm, thus avoiding the international complications that might have resulted from a straightforward government-to-government contract."

11. For example, see Reinsch to Lansing, 10 December 1918, 893.51/2079, FRUS 1918, pp. 197-98.

12. Jordan to Curzon, 20 January 1919, F.O. 371/3682, 59956, PRO. In concluding his telegram to London, Jordan offered an interesting perspective on the possible motivation of Japan's China policy: "Mr. Obata probably believes, and could quote the authority of the *Times* to support his belief, that China is as surely doomed to succumb to the forcible impact of modern civilization as the Red Man was doomed by the White Man's discovery of America, and it is only on such assumption that Japanese policy in this country becomes intelligible."

13. See the minutes under Jordan to Balfour, 5 February 1919, F.O. 371/3682, 21634, and 6 February 1919, F.O. 371/3682, 22356, PRO. See also Chan, *Arming the Chinese*, p. 16.

14. Iriye noted that "within the United States official and non-official suspicion of Japan reached a new climax during 1918-1921 despite Japanese protestation of their desire for understanding," *Across the Pacific*, p. 139.

15. Jordan to Curzon, 11 February 1919, F.O. 371/3682, 52969, PRO. Two weeks later Jordan reiterated similar thoughts in a letter to Lord Bryce: "The collapse of Russia and Germany has put an end to imperialistic aggression from those quarters but the Japanese menace is much nearer and more serious." 25 February 1919, F.O. 350/16.

16. Reinsch to Lansing, 24 February 1919, 893.00/3021, FRUS 1919, p. 300. On 13 February Minister Greene in Tokyo was instructed to inform the Japanese government of the "considerable apprehension" with which London viewed the status of Chinese affairs. Balfour to Greene, 13 February 1919, F.O. 371/3682, 23010, PRO. After a discussion with the British chargé

in Washington, Breckenridge Long wrote that London's telegram to Greene "showed the development of rather a serious situation and a considerable degree of apprehension existing in the minds of the British Minister at Peking and the British Ambassador at Tokyo, and a corresponding reflection in the attitude of the British Government." Memorandum dated 17 February 1919, 893.51/2117.5, DSNA. The next day, Polk told Chargé d'Affaires MacMurray in Tokyo that "this Government views . . . an addition to the military forces of China with considerable alarm and apprehension." Polk to MacMurray, 18 February 1919, 893.51/2117.5, FRUS 1919, p. 298.

17. Reinsch to Lansing, 26 February 1919, 893.00/2963, DSNA.

18. Greene to Balfour, 17 February 1919, F.O. 371/3682, 27210, PRO.

19. Balfour to Jordan, 24 February 1919, F.O. 371/3682, 28688, PRO.

20. Although the Japanese had attempted to minimize the importance of Tuan's army within China by stating that only officers had so far been recruited for it, high-ranking Chinese informed Jordan that between ten thousand and thirty thousand men were actually under arms. See Greene to Balfour, 17 February 1919, F.O. 371/3682, 27210, Jordan to Balfour, 22 February 1919, F.O. 371/3682, 30028, and Jordan to Balfour, 2 March 1919, F.O. 371/3682, 34900, PRO.

21. Jordan to Balfour, 24 February 1919, F.O. 371/3682, 31421, PRO. In the same telegram, Jordan expressed the opinion that there was little prospect of reunification so long as the military regime in the North received the support of Japan. In order to alter the state of affairs, he believed that the "best means to that end would be [the] presence of adequate naval forces in Chinese waters, coupled with genuine and united intimation from [the] Allies that [the] present state of things could no longer be tolerated."

22. MacMurray to Lansing, 28 February 1919, 893.51/2133, FRUS 1919, p. 303.

23. For the text of this note, see Reinsch to Lansing, 7 March 1919, 893.00/3049, FRUS 1919, p. 311.

24. Within the Foreign Office, W. G. Max Muller wrote that such arguments "confirm the prevalent impression that it is not in their [Japan's] real interest to promote the reestablishment of peace in China. The representation suggested by us could only be resented by the Northern militarists, who are supported by Japanese funds and would certainly not be regarded by the President or by the Southern party as undue interference in China's internal affairs." Minute under Jordan to Balfour, 4 March 1919, F.O. 371/3682, 36157, PRO.

25. Jordan to Curzon, 4 March 1919, F.O. 371/3682, 62492, PRO. Reinsch explained to Washington that Tokyo would not mind such an outcome: "Early success in [the] Shanghai peace conference would not be favorable to the Japanese. National unity restored will deprive of power [the] clique which without national authority has used the central government [organization?] to make deals with Japan. Effective national [organization?] in [China] would prevent these unconscionable arrangements [from] yielding permanent results as is shown by [the] indignant protests raised against them throughout China. The Japanese do not therefore desire at the present time to see China reorganized and her credit strengthened. The present state of disorganization enables them to extend still further their influence over [individuals?] and consolidate the military faction." Reinsch to Lansing, 29 March 1919, 893.0/2995, DSNA.

26. Reinsch to Lansing, 11 March 1919, 893.00/3043, DSNA. Reinsch and Jordan did consider the embarrassing possibility that an arms embargo might ultimately work to the advantage of Tokyo; since Tuan had received nearly two years of support from Japan, an arms embargo could hinder southern forces, which had not been so supplied and which would be cut off from outside sources. After discussing this issue, both Reinsch and Jordan concluded that regardless of the possible short-term consequences, the long-range impact of the arms embargo would be beneficial. See Reinsch to Lansing, 5 April 1919, 693.119/420, FRUS 1919, p. 667. Initially Reinsch had wanted to permit the South to receive arms and ammunition from abroad, but Jordan convinced him of the necessity of a complete embargo. See Jordan to Balfour, 27 March 1919, F.O. 371/3682, 50782, PRO.

27. Reinsch to Lansing, 11 March 1919, 893.00/3043, DSNA.

28. Jordan to Balfour, 4 March 1919, F.O. 371/3682, 35686 and 11 March 1919, F.O. 371/3682, 40939, PRO. On 19 March the Foreign Office approved Jordan's position, and instructed him to continue pressing for the disbandment of the War Participation Army. See Balfour to Jordan, 19 March 1919, F.O. 371/3682, 41863, PRO.

29. Reinsch to Lansing, 13 March 1919, 893.51/2148, FRUS 1919, pp. 321-22.

30. Reinsch to Lansing, 27 March 1919, 893.00/3062, DSNA. It is interesting to note that these sentences were the only two omitted from the telegram as recorded on pages 322-27 of FRUS 1919. Appended to this document in the State Department archives was a note of 22 April from Nelson T. Johnson to Miller, in which he stated that "it seems to me that if

we have evidence enough of double dealing on the part of Japan in the general policy of the associated powers in Chinese affairs it is high time that notice was served upon Japan that it is time to put a stop to such policies especially since in her action, Japan is really committing us as well as the Allied powers to a policy of giving support to one Chinese faction as against another."

31. Minute under Balfour to Jordan, 15 March 1919, F.O. 371/3682, 41713, PRO.

32. Jordan to Balfour, 27 March 1919, F.O. 371/3682, 50782, PRO.

33. Obata to Reinsch, 2 April 1919, 693.119/268, DSNA.

34. Reinsch to Obata, 3 April 1919, 693.119/268, DSNA.

35. Reinsch to Lansing, 4 April 1919, 693.119/268, DSNA.

36. See Reinsch to Lansing, 10 May 1919, 693.119/273, FRUS 1919, pp. 669-70.

37. Polk to Reinsch, 14 April 1919, 693.119/421, FRUS 1919, p. 668.

5

Challenges to the China Arms Embargo

During the first months of 1919, while the diplomats in Peking finally hammered together the China arms embargo, the Versailles Peace Conference captured world attention. Many Chinese regarded the Paris deliberations as a forum at which to air grievances in the hope of improving China's status vis-à-vis the great powers. Ultimately, the question of the return of Shantung province, the former German possession that Japan had occupied and administered during the war, became the symbol of China's quest for full national sovereignty.

Word of the decision to permit continued Japanese possession of Shantung reached China in early May 1919. Popular dissatisfaction with the news sparked a series of demonstrations and a boycott of Japanese goods known as the May 4 Movement.[1] One effect of the Shantung decision was to alienate further the northern regime from a civilian population which already perceived Peking officials as being pro-Japanese.

The northern warlords, however, were shaken neither by these signs of internal unrest, nor by international displeasure as manifested by the loan ban and arms embargo. Reinsch reported in the middle of June that the so-called Anfu clique,[2] comprised of warlords closely associated with Japan, still controlled Peking and continued to receive Japanese encouragement. General Hsü Shu-cheng now exercised immediate control of the Anfu Club because Tuan Ch'i-jui, although repeatedly urged to place himself at the head of the organization, refused to have any formal connection with it.[3]

Peking's refusal to be cowed was only one cause of frustration for the powers sponsoring the arms embargo. Unfortunately, the concurrence of Washington, London, and Tokyo on the necessity to impose an arms embargo on China was not sufficient to ensure that all other countries would fall in line and adhere to the agreement. Challenges to the embargo's integrity occurred almost from the very start.

Italy posed the first threat. Although the Italian minister in Peking expressed personal sympathy with the aims of the embargo, Rome instructed him on 15 May 1919 to make an exception for war materials already contracted for but not yet delivered to China. Reinsch immediately took alarm at the Italian position, not because of the amount of weaponry involved, but rather "if [the] Italians persist, it is feared that other Powers will feel that they cannot justly restrict their own citizens."[4] Reinsch was obviously concerned that the Japanese would seize upon the Italian disposition and use it as a pretext to justify the completion of the Taihei contract to Tuan's forces. Acting Secretary of State Polk reacted promptly, instructing the ambassador in Rome to request that the Italian government withdraw its exception. Polk also asked Reinsch to confer with his colleagues in Peking in order to convince the Italian minister that uniform action in China was essential.[5] Over the next few weeks, both the British and French governments agreed with the American position.[6]

The central question was not, however, the Italian response, but rather that of the Japanese. Indeed, Jordan for a time even believed that Tokyo and Rome were coordinating their efforts to undermine the agreement. He thought it significant that both the Japanese and Italian ministers had requested fresh instructions from their home governments after Peking had protested the embargo on the grounds that: (1) the peace treaty officially ending World War I was not yet signed; (2) military operations against the enemy were not completed; and (3) that the bolshevik presence on the Russian frontier remained a menace. In dismissing these Chinese arguments as "absurd," Jordan warned on 6 July that, with respect to the recent Italian and Japanese actions, "it is not unreasonable to infer that there may be collusion between them."[7] Jordan's suspicions, however, were unwarranted; the next day he was "glad" to report that the Japanese minister had informed him that Tokyo considered it "absolutely necessary to adhere strictly to [the] existing arrangement about [the] prohibition of [the] import of arms and ammunition."[8] At least for the moment the Japanese refrained from taking advantage of the Italian position in order to press for a modification of the embargo.

With Japan giving diplomatic support to the embargo, the powers awaited Rome's response. The Italians gave the powers an early indication of their embargo diplomacy with Rome's initial reaction to the American, British, and French inquiries. On 12 June 1919 Jordan reported that the Italian minister had already awaited instructions from Rome for some three weeks. The Italian minister and his successors were to wait much longer; five months later, at the request of the French government, the State Department instructed the ambassador in Rome to make renewed representations along with his French colleague to the Italian government if it seemed appropriate to do so.[9] Still three months later, in February 1920, Acting Secretary of State Polk asked the embassy in Rome to report the results of the various representations to the Italian government. The chargé replied that the French Embassy had never broached the subject of the embargo with the American Embassy, although the French ambassador had made a separate representation to the Italians in December 1919. The chargé had, however, learned from informal conversations at the Foreign Office that the "reason no official reply has been given was owing to [the] absence from Peking of [the] Italian Minister who is alone considered competent to settle this question which . . . required careful protection of Italian interests and that pending [the] arrival of [the] Minister no official reply could be safely made to either the French or our communication."[10] While it was true that the forces of Gabriele d'Annunzio temporarily detained the new Italian minister to Peking in Fiume, the chargé admitted that the heart of the problem was that the "Italian Government being so interested in matters nearer home apparently pays little attention to the matter [of evading the embargo]." The chargé chose not to take issue with Rome over the delay, since an imminent reply was expected.[11]

The Italian tactics were similar to those of the Japanese government when the Taihei contract was under discussion in the winter of 1918-1919. In both cases the offending party made arms deliveries while diplomatically stalling for time. There were, however, several glaring differences between the two cases. First of all, when presented with united opposition to its aid-Tuan policy, the Japanese government had vigorously defended its position in diplomatic circles. The Italians, when faced with similar opposition to their reservation regarding the arms embargo, adopted a stance of silent delay. The second difference was that the Japanese contracts dwarfed those of the Italians. Finally, and most significantly, while Japan's shipments had clear political overtones, Rome could only dream of playing such a role in the Far East. Instead, the Italians had to content themselves with merely the monetary profit from their arms contracts.

In and of themselves, the Italian arms sales were really only a nuisance. Secretary Polk made this clear in a memorandum to the British chargé in Washington on 13 March 1920: "In so far as the question of Italy is concerned . . . the information of this Government does not indicate such activity in the arms traffic on the part of Italians as would jeopardize the purposes of the embargo or warrant its discontinuance at the present time."[12] The Italians did, however, give critics continuing examples of the embargo's weaknesses and provided ammunition to those who wanted to wreck the agreement.

While Italy's tactics tested the patience of American, British, and Japanese diplomats, the embargo nonetheless did deprive the Chinese of weapons from the world's major suppliers. Yet initially there were few visible changes in the Chinese situation. At the end of June 1919 Jordan acknowledged that some six weeks after the formation of the embargo:

We have succeeded in prohibiting [the] importation of arms and munitions of war, have stopped ruinous Japanese loans and have otherwise done what is possible to maintain [a] semblance of government. But all these are negative measures and afford no permanent remedy. Japanese money is no longer forthcoming but [the] military monster which it has helped to create and support must continue to feed on something unless means can be formed to disband it.[13]

Jordan and Reinsch believed that financial support to President Hsü Shih-ch'ang, for both the disbandment of troops and financial reform, was essential in order to facilitate an immediate change in Chinese affairs.[14]

But neither Tokyo nor the Peking warlords were interested in an alteration of the status quo in China. In order to prevent the Consortium from making a loan to President Hsü's government, Japan proceeded to drag out the negotiations trying to put the Consortium together.[15] At the same time, the northern military party in China also opposed the workings of the Consortium.

Increasingly discouraged, President Hsü sent an urgent message to Reinsch at the end of August 1919, in which he expressed his belief that General Hsü was strongly working against China's acceptance of any loans from the Consortium. The president feared that unless funds were forthcoming, his government would be overthrown and the military would dominate the whole country with Japanese assistance.[16] Ironically Washington and London now found that the loan ban prevented action; because of it they could not give aid to the Chinese civilians trying to end the military's dominant position within the country.

Since independent loans to China were not possible, Reinsch told the State Department that one way to rehabilitate American prestige in China was to push through the Consortium negotiations without delay. Furthermore, if the Japanese succeeded in wrecking the Consortium, he urged that the United States then give financial assistance to China either unilaterally or with other powers. Reinsch warned that if President Hsü received no outside funding, "the position which the United States has been building up the past few years as a Power actively interested in China will be lost and she will again be relegated by popular opinion to the position of a benevolent but impotent spectator."[17]

Washington chose not to take Reinsch's advice and as a consequence, China's financial crisis deepened. By the fall of 1919, bloated by military expenses, Chinese governmental expenditures exceeded revenues by ten million dollars per month.[18] Such a situation was made even worse because the military generally insisted on having its obligations met before those of the administrative branches.

In order to survive, the Chinese government adopted what Reinsch termed "extreme measures" to secure funds. These included numerous short-term loans with native banks at a heavy discount and at interest rates as high as 2.5 percent a month.[19] Thus the ban on foreign loans, as well as the arms embargo, made it increasingly difficult for Peking to maintain, let alone expand, the armed forces on which it depended for survival. Clearly, Peking would be in serious trouble once domestic sources of money were exhausted, and Jordan reported to London that he and his American and French colleagues agreed that the "financial strain which they [the military] have imposed upon [the] country must sooner or later bring about collapse."[20]

Peking officials, in their search to delay financial disaster, very nearly found an unlikely source of money: London. In order to understand why the British contemplated circumventing the loan ban, and then ultimately violated the spirit of the arms embargo, it is necessary to recall that Great Britain, as well as the other major powers, faced great reductions in armament industries at the end of World War I. Specifically, if commercial markets could not be found for the young aircraft industry, cuts in production could lead to the dispersal of skilled technicians, which might hamper future military preparedness. Thus the development of a peacetime trade in aircraft could eliminate several potential problems.[21]

Some two months before the powers agreed to impose an arms embargo on China, a British concern, the Peking Syndicate, concluded a contract to sell six British-made Handley Page airplanes to the Aviation Department of the Chinese government's Board of Communications.   Soon thereafter, Handley Page's rival, Vickers Limited, began negotiations for a much larger deal, involving one hundred commercial-type planes and spare parts.[22]

Although the Department of Overseas Trade vigorously advocated securing the Chinese aviation market for British industry, the Foreign Office nonetheless still sought the opinion of Sir John Jordan. In informing Jordan of the Vickers negotiations on 29 July 1919, Foreign Secretary Marquess Curzon of Kedleston emphasized that the contract called for a cash advance of £500,000 to China in order "to enable [the] Chinese Govt. [sic] to utilize [the] machines."   Curzon remarked that: "Before proceeding further we should like to have your observations on the proposed transaction, especially as to how far the issue of such a loan would conflict with the agreement suspending further advances to the Chinese Govt. [sic] pending the reestablishment of order in China."[23]   Jordan promptly questioned the wisdom of the Vickers agreement, replying: "Our attitude will be open to criticism here in the event of Treasury sanction for [a] loan of £500,000. . . . I fear it will be very difficult to convince Chinese and foreign critics [that] the money will be used for legitimate purposes."[24]   Indeed, the financially strapped Peking government looked upon aircraft contracts more as a method to obtain foreign money than as a way to begin civil aviation.[25]   The Chinese ultimately would not receive much money from the British contract, but it caused London much grief from the other powers.[26]

Jordan also pointed out yet another weakness in the plan to sell Vickers aircraft to China: Peking apparently sought to use some of the planes in a military expedition against Mongolia.[27]   Such a flagrant evasion of the arms embargo could easily result in the complete breakdown of the agreement. In spite of Jordan's observations, London eventually decided to try to secure the China market for the British aviation industry; it would, however, at the same time attempt to avoid wrecking the embargo by seeking assurances that planes shipped to China were of a commercial type and would not be used for military purposes.   London would also attempt to justify the aviation contract on the grounds that the embargo, which applied to "arms, ammunition and munitions of war," did not include "commercial" aircraft.

The British attitude toward the sale of commercial aircraft to China raised the question of what exactly the powers had agreed to embargo in May 1919.   The problems stemming from aircraft shipments to China demonstrated clearly that technological change had blurred the distinction between civilian and military materials. This uncertainty over what did or did not constitute arms, ammunition and munitions of war, however, was not confined solely to finished products such as airplanes. In August 1919 the Chinese government had inquired whether the arms embargo included raw materials for the manufacture of weaponry. The State Department informed Reinsch that Washington included not only raw materials for the manufacture of weaponry, but also the machinery used in its manufacture.[28] Given London's role in the formation of the embargo, Washington assumed that the British position on the scope of the agreement would be as extensive as its own.

Word of the Vickers contract therefore came as an unpleasant surprise to American officials. On 17 November 1919 Lansing instructed the American ambassador in London to ask whether or not the British government had actually approved the contract and to "inform the British Government that this Government has placed the broadest interpretation possible upon this understanding even to the extent of discouraging contracts by American firms for machinery and raw materials used in the manufacture of munitions, and ask what interpretation the British Government has placed thereon."[29] The British reply did little to allay American suspicions. On the one hand, the Foreign Office declared that London's interpretation of the embargo was the same as Washington's. But on the other hand, the Foreign Office defended the Vickers contract on the grounds that "the agreement was for a credit loan the proceeds of which are to be spent in Great Britain on commercial aeronautical material wholly unsuited for any military purpose whatsoever."[30] The British attitude left Washington in an awkward position; American bankers and aircraft manufacturers could charge that State Department laxness had allowed British concerns to conclude a lucrative contract without competition from the United States. Furthermore, the Vickers contract drove a wedge between the two powers most interested in maintaining a united front on the embargo.

Behind the Anglo-American disagreement over commercial aircraft, the problem of Japan's response worried diplomats in both London and Washington. Throughout the summer and fall of 1919 there were rumors of Japanese violations of the arms embargo, but extensive investigation failed to discover any evidence to support these allegations.[31] On 18 October, however, Jordan reported that he learned on good authority that the Japanese concern Mitsui Bussan Kaisha was negotiating a $1.5 million contract to deliver arsenal machinery and to construct a smokeless powder plant in Canton. He believed that these negotiations had been undertaken with Tokyo's connivance.[32]

Ambassador Beilby Alston in Tokyo asked both the naval attaché and military attaché to make inquiries regarding Jordan's telegram. For their part, the Japanese assured the British that no such contract existed,[33] and Alston surmised that the project might have emanated from the Mitsui Bussan Kaisha agent in Canton, who acted independently of his superiors in the hope of promotion if the deal went through.[34]

Alston also warned London that the numerous inaccurate reports of Japanese violations of the arms embargo had strained relations with Tokyo:

> The Military Attaché is informed at the War Office that the Japanese Authorities are getting seriously annoyed at the constant enquiries into reports emanating from China which upon investigation prove to be without foundation, but which none the less impute bad faith on their part and lack of confidence on ours.
>
> It is of course most undesirable that we should give offence to the War Office Authorities unnecessarily, but the Japanese have, justly or unjustly, earned such a reputation for underhand methods that I am afraid any story to their disadvantage nowadays is credited, whether it is supported by proof or not. It is in fact a case of a dog with a bad name. . . .
>
> I hope this will not be interpreted as meaning that I am prepared to vouch for the accuracy of Japanese official denials; I am unfortunately not in a position to do anything of the kind, having none too profound a faith in them.[35]

Not only had the inaccurate accusations irritated Tokyo, but more than one British official was aware that the Vickers contract placed Great Britain on shaky ground. Jordan, in suggesting inquires be made into the Mitsui Bussan Kaisha case on 18 October, had confessed the fear that the "conclusion of [the] Vickers Aeroplane contract may weaken our position vis-à-vis [the] other powers and [with respect to the] munitions embargo generally."[36] In the minute under this telegram, one Foreign Office official reflected Jordan's uneasiness by writing that the "Vickers contract is, technically at least, quite entirely defensible" and then crossed out the word "entirely."[37]

Four days after Jordan's telegram concerning the rumored Mitsui Bussan Kaisha contract, the Japanese minister at Peking did indeed question him about the Vickers contract. After Jordan defended the deal by declaring that the planes "were in no way suitable for military purposes," the Japanese minister countered with the remark that the "only Chinese employed on aviation [were] military men."[38] Jordan recorded no direct reply to the Japanese minister's implication that Britain had violated the embargo.

Although the Japanese minister ultimately expressed satisfaction with Jordan's explanations concerning the Vickers contract and loan, Tokyo apparently was not so easily persuaded. On 1 November the counsellor of the Japanese Embassy in London requested further clarification regarding the Vickers loan.[39]

The Japanese did not, however, content themselves merely with quiet diplomatic inquiries into the airplane question; in the middle of November 1919 Alston reported that the Japanese press had joined the fray. He suggested that a combination of three factors: (1) the possibility of an independent $25 million gold loan to China from U.S. financiers, (2) Rome's apparently partly successful effort to fulfill its arms contracts with China, and (3) the Vickers contract, had together "combined to furnish some of the Japanese newspapers with an apposite text for the delivering of a brief series of homilies on the subject of Western political immorality."[40] Alston drew particular attention to the opinions presented in the *Kokumin Shimbun*, a newspaper with close ties to the War Office and General Staff, and generally believed to represent both the military and the bureaucratic castes in Japan. He concluded his despatch by pointing out that in spite of British statements to the contrary, a presumably well informed paper like *Kokumin* still regarded the Vickers contract as a loan made for military and not commercial purposes. The Japanese, however, as yet chose to stay their hand and did not make an official representation to London for another six weeks; during this period the Japanese ambassador to Rome even protested recent Italian arms shipments to China along with his British and French colleagues.[41]

The Japanese finally acted on 30 December 1919, when Minister for Foreign Affairs Uchida Yasuya sent Alston the note that British officials had long anticipated. Uchida maintained that since February 1919, Tokyo had faithfully and sincerely enforced the arms embargo, thereby causing "considerable losses" and "unspeakable hardships" to Japanese merchants. Concerning Japan's grievances, specifically the Vickers contract and Italian arms sales, Uchida piously expressed that "it would, of course, be difficult to take back the Italian arms and British aeroplanes already delivered to the Chinese, and accordingly, with regard to these the Imperial Government does not wish to pursue the matter further."[42] Tokyo was not, however, willing to forget and forgive these alleged transgressions. Rather the Japanese asked for reciprocity and desired to export the remaining portion of the Taihei contracts to China. As a concession to British sensibilities the Japanese did offer to establish some method of control to ensure that this weaponry would not be turned over to the Chinese until the North and South had reconciled their differences. This was, however, an empty gesture, since the Chinese would first have to agree to it.[43]

The Foreign Office was greatly alarmed at the prospect of the possible completion of the Taihei contracts, which would have been "little short of disastrous."[44] London adopted a threefold strategy in order to placate Tokyo. First of all, the British implied that the Japanese request was inconsistent, since Tokyo had just a month before lodged an official protest in Rome because of Italian violations of the arms embargo. The Foreign Office also reiterated its position that the Vickers aircraft were intended for bona fide commercial purposes and that the Japanese minister in Peking had previously expressed his satisfaction with Jordan's explanations to that effect. Finally, London informed Tokyo that the British government had detained in Hong Kong a consignment of munitions worth $500,000 intended for the Canton government, and had also refused to sell dismantled warships to China. The British pointed out that while His Majesty's Government could have profited from a revision of the arms policy, London opposed such a move and hoped that the Japanese would continue to adhere to the embargo because of its "absolute necessity."[45]

The British defense of the embargo succeeded. When Alston met with Uchida on 20 January 1920, the British ambassador emphasized that although more numerous, Japanese merchants were no worse off than their counterparts in England who were not allowed to deliver arms to China. Alston also took the initiative and asked Uchida for suggestions to bring Italy into line on the embargo. Uchida's only "solution" was to permit the Japanese to deliver their shipments, which Alston did not treat as a serious proposal. At the meeting Uchida took no action other than to promise to reexamine the Vickers situation, and the Japanese note of 30 December was forgotten.[46]

Thus the China arms embargo survived its first major challenge; the Japanese, having aired their grievances, apparently continued to honor the agreement.[47] In spite of various problems, Jordan was confident that the embargo was worth the effort: "There may be and doubtless are, infringements of [the] embargo, and Messrs. Vickers' aeroplane contract has been severely criticized in this respect. But [the] maintenance of [the] embargo has [the] wholehearted support of [?entire] Chinese public opinion [?and its] application to loans also [?is] warmly advocated by almost [the] whole press in China."[48] Jordan could not know that within six months, in spite of renewed attacks on the embargo's integrity, the policy would be vindicated with Tuan's downfall.

NOTES

1. One can get an idea of the extent of the anti-Japanese sentiment among the Chinese by noting that the boycott was still effective four months later. In commenting on a summary of Chinese consular intelligence reports, H. P. Brune minuted in September 1919 that "this is, on the whole, a dismal record--civil discord, brigandage and opium, all as bad as ever. The bright spot is the Japanese boycott, which has been maintained with energy and success in practically every district." Minute of H. P. Brune under Jordan to Balfour, 13 September 1919, F.O. 371/3701, 151237, PRO.

2. Reinsch to Lansing, 4 July 1919, 893.00/3151.5, DSNA. With respect to this name, Reinsch told Washington that "'Anfu' [represented] a combination of *An*hwei, the province of the militarists, and *Fu*kien, the province of the naval people [emphasis in original]." Reinsch to Lansing, 10 September 1919, 893.00/3235, FRUS 1919, p. 360.

3. Reinsch to Lansing, 10 September 1919, 893.00/3235, FRUS 1919, p. 361. Reinsch believed that General Hsü was actively involved in planning "an indefinite establishment of the Chino-Japanese [*sic*] Military Convention, applying it more specifically to the Northwestern frontier regions--that it will involve the creation of a Chinese military force under Japanese instructors and officers; that this force with Japanese military and financial support may eventually be used to enforce the domination of the Peking pro-Japanese military clique against resisting forces in China and thus to result in a military protectorate exercised by Japan." For this quotation see DSNA.

4. Reinsch to Lansing, 19 May 1919, 693.119/276, DSNA.

5. See Polk to Page, 20 May 1919; and Polk to Reinsch, 21 May 1919, 693.119/271, FRUS 1919, p. 671.

6. See Balfour to Jordan, 6 June, 1919, FO 371/3683, 84708; Jordan to Balfour, 7 June 1919, F.O. 371/3683, 85951; and Jordan to Balfour, 12 June 1919, F.O. 371/3683, 88086, PRO.

7. Jordan to Balfour, 6 July 1919, F.O. 371/3683, 100961, PRO.

8. Jordan to Balfour, 7 July 1919, F.O. 371/3683, 100962, PRO.

9. Lansing to Page, 28 November 1919, 693.119/289, FRUS 1919,

pp. 673-74.

10. Jay to Polk, 18 February 1920, 693.119/306, FRUS 1920, p. 740.

11. Ibid., p. 741. The chargé was mistaken; not until July would Minister Charles Crane report from Peking that the "Italian Legation publishes [a] statement that [the] Italian Government has not agreed not to sell military supplies in China; that when [the] embargo was agreed upon [the] Italian Government made [a] reservation of unfulfilled contracts and that it is no longer able and willing to postpone execution of certain contracts." Crane to Polk, 13 July 1920, 693.119/334, FRUS 1920, pp. 440-41.

12. Polk to Lindsay, 13 March 1920, 693.119/303, FRUS 1920, p. 742. Italian obstruction was not confined only to the arms embargo, but to financial matters as well. During the Consortium negotiations in the summer of 1919, the United States, Great Britain, Japan, and France decided to release a small amount of money from customs funds to both Chinese governments. Only the Italians dissented. Minister Garbasso informed the Diplomatic Corps that Italian consent hinged upon a satisfactory settlement of the Passari case, in which the Italian liquidator of the Deutsch-Asiatische Bank at Shanghai had put forward a large claim for commission. Jordan believed that the Italian action was "absolutely indefensible" and refused to "be associated with such a scandal." As dean of the Diplomatic Corps, and with the assent of his other colleagues, Jordan authorized the release of the customs funds. Jordan informed London that "the action of Monsieur Garbasso has succeeded in breaking up the solidarity of the Diplomatic Body, a most regrettable result and occurring for the first time in my experience. It has always been the rule to act by unanimity: but in the present instance it was out of the question that the honor of the whole Diplomatic Body should be compromised owing to the folly of a Minister having just nine weeks experience of Chinese affairs and no scruples. . . . During his short stay here he [Garbasso] has displayed a most unwelcome activity and a tendency to make trouble unnecessarily." See Jordan to Balfour, 2 July 1919, F.O. 371/3683, 118931 and 97670, PRO. It is tempting to attribute Great Britain's subsequent refusal to allow an Italian group into the Consortium to Rome's uncooperative China policy in 1919. However, more influential in the Consortium decision were the considerations that "Italy has practically no financial or industrial interests in China and there is a danger that any Italian group which might be formed for the purpose would be under German influence." Minute of Ronald Macleay under Lord Hardinge to Curzon, 24 September 1919, F.O. 371/3683, 134241, PRO.

13. Jordan to Curzon, 23 June 1919, F.O. 371/3695, 93198, PRO.

14. Ibid. In advising Washington of the need to provide financial support to President Hsü, Reinsch warned that "unless the United States and the powers can give attention to this situation it will crystallize in a manner that will leave the Far East a source of great danger. Prevention will be infinitely easier than the cure." Reinsch to Polk, 12 July 1919, 893.00/3167, and Reinsch to Polk, 4 July 1919, 893.00/3151.5, DSNA.

15. See Reinsch to Lansing, 26 June 1919, 893.51/2284; 2 July 1919, 893.51/2293; and 11 July 1919, 893.51/2310, FRUS 1919, pp. 458-65. Jordan to Curzon, 12 February 1920, 178796/8369/10, *Documents on British Foreign Policy, 1919-1939*, E. L. Woodward and Rohan Butler, eds. (London: 1956) 1st ser., vol. 6, p. 993 (hereafter cited as DBFP).

16. Reinsch to Polk, 30 August 1919, 893.00/3210, DSNA.

17. Reinsch to Polk, 10 September 1919, 893.00/3235, FRUS 1919, p. 369.

18. Reinsch to Lansing, 10 September 1919, 893.00/3235, DSNA.

19. Ibid.

20. Jordan to Balfour, 23 June 1919, F.O. 371/3695, 93198, PRO.

21. Noel Pugach, "Anglo-American Aircraft Competition and the China Arms Embargo, 1919-1921," *Diplomatic History*, 2, no. 4 (Fall 1978): 351. In this article Pugach provides an excellent analysis of the causes and consequences of the Anglo-American aircraft competition in China.

22. Ibid., p. 354.

23. Curzon to Jordan, 29 July 1919, 104790/93224/10, DBFP, 1st ser., vol. 6, p. 651.

24. Jordan to Curzon, 29 July 1919, 110424/93224/10, DBFP, 1st ser., vol. 6, pp. 651-52.

25. Certainly this was the case late in 1920 when Handley Page negotiated a contract to sell 105 flying boats and hydroplanes to the Peking government. Significantly this contract, which included a £400,000 advance to the government, was not concluded with the Aeronautics Department, but with the Ministry of Finance, which needed funds to pay its short-term loans to domestic creditors on the Chinese New Year. See Pugach, "Aircraft," pp. 354-57.

26. The Vickers loan was structured so as to ensure that most of the money was spent in England, and the British Legation in Peking refused to register the 1920 Handley Page contract. See Curzon to Jordan, 15 August 1919, 116004/93224/10, DBFP, 1st ser., vol. 6, p. 680; and Beilby Alston to Curzon, 27 December 1920, F.O. 371/5927, F 3421/1/10, PRO.

27. Jordan to Curzon, 29 July 1919, 110424/93224/10, DBFP, 1st ser., vol. 6, pp. 651-52.

28. See Reinsch to Lansing, 30 August 1919; and Philips to Reinsch, 10 September, 693.119/281, FRUS 1919, p. 672.

29. Lansing to Davis, 17 November 1919, 693.119/289, FRUS 1919, p. 672.

30. Davis to Lansing, 22 November 1919, 893.51/2552, FRUS 1919, p. 673. Unfortunately for the Foreign Office, in China every airplane could be used for war purposes. As the head of Vickers admitted to one Foreign Office official "a bomb can be easily thrown from any aeroplane." Minute of Sir John Tilley under Jordan to Curzon, 24 January 1920, F.O. 371/3684, 174383/391/10, PRO. In defending the commercial nature of the aircraft it sold to China, Vickers Limited argued that the airplanes "stand in the same relation to war material as motor-cars, railway wagons or merchant steamers, none of which are intended as such, though all could be used for transport of troops or munitions and possibly, with some modification, for offensive purposes." See Alston to Curzon, 13 January 1920, F.O. 371/3684, 170856, PRO.

31. Alston to Curzon, 17 November 1919, 165586/394/10, DBFP, 1st ser., vol. 6, p. 834.

32. See Jordan to Curzon, 18 October 1919, which is printed in note 1 under Jordan to Curzon, 22 October 1919, 145713/93224/10, DBFP, 1st ser., vol. 6, p. 794.

33. One official in the Foreign Office minuted that "these assurances sound satisfactory." Minute of H. P. Brune, under Alston to Curzon, 7 November 1919, F.O. 371/3683, 150857, PRO.

34. Alston to Curzon, 17 November 1919, 165586/394/10, DBFP, 1st ser., vol. 6, p. 833.

35. Ibid. p. 834. Alston hoped that in the future, rumors of Japanese violations of the embargo would be more rigorously investigated before being brought to the attention of Tokyo.

36. Jordan to Curzon, 18 October 1919, which is printed in note 1 under Jordan to Curzon, 22 October 1919, 145713/93224/10, DBFP, 1st ser., vol. 6, p. 794. By February 1920 Jordan confessed that "I have always felt we were on thin ice in regard to this contract but did not feel justified in saying more than I did in view of [the] evident desire of His Majesty's Government that it should go through in the interest of British trade." Jordan to Curzon, 19 February 1920, 182163/394/10, DBFP, 1st ser., vol. 6, p. 1005.

37. See the Brune minute under Jordan to Curzon, 18 October 1919,

F.O. 371/3683, 143859/394/10, PRO.

38. Jordan to Curzon, 22 October 1919, 145713/93224/10, DBFP, 1st ser., vol. 6, pp. 794-95.

39. Memorandum of Max Muller, 1 November 1919, 148494/39224/10, DBFP, 1st ser., vol. 6, p. 815. See also note 1.

40. Alston to Curzon, 18 November 1919, 166691/8369/10, DBFP, 1st ser., vol. 6, pp. 835-37.

41. Buchanan to Curzon, 15 December 1919, F.O. 371/3684, 165455, PRO.

42. This communication is summarized in Alston to Curzon, 2 January 1920, 167562/394/10, DBFP, 1st ser., vol. 6, pp. 916-17.

43. Ibid.

44. Hardinge to Alston, 10 January 1920, 167562/394/10, DBFP, 1st ser., vol. 6, pp. 927-28.

45. Ibid., p. 928.

46. Alston to Curzon, 21 January 1920, F.O. 371/3684, 173660, PRO.

47. Alan Archer, the vice-consul at Tsingtao, reported to Jordan in February 1920 that "it has frequently been stated in the press and elsewhere that the Japanese carry on and encourage [the] import of arms into China. . . . In spite, however, of every effort having been made by His Majesty's Consul General at Tsinaufu and others to prove the truth of these allegations or to ascertain the methods adopted, no single concrete case has ever been produced in evidence." See Jordan to Curzon, 25 February 1920, F.O. 371/5295, F 480/1/10, PRO. In May 1920 the American chargé d'affaires also indicated he could find no evidence of Japanese arms shipments. Tenney to Colby, 17 May 1920, 693.119/320, FRUS 1920, p. 743.

48. Jordan to Curzon, 18 February 1920, F.O. 371/3684, 181821, PRO.

6

The Success of the China Arms Embargo

In March 1920 Sir John Jordan left the Far East to return to England and begin his retirement after fourteen years as His Majesty's Minister at Peking. Before leaving, one of Jordan's last duties was to write an annual report summarizing Chinese affairs for 1919. In it he offered the opinion that, on the whole, the concerned parties had faithfully observed the arms embargo. He also expressed the belief that this prohibition had "undoubtedly exercised a great influence on the situation."[1] Jordan and Reinsch could indeed take pride in the instrument because four months later, the principal goal of the China arms embargo would be achieved: the defeat of Tuan Ch'i-jui's forces and the ouster of his pro-Japanese clique from power.

The overthrow of the Anfu party did not directly originate in China's North-South conflict, but rather from a dispute within the northern regime itself. In the spring of 1920 Anfu General Hsü Shu-cheng initiated the crisis when he proposed to establish a new army division for service in Outer Mongolia. Such a move portended not only the strengthening of the pro-Japanese Anfu party by expanding its armed forces, but the extension of Japanese influence into Mongolia as well. The governor general of Manchuria, General Chang Tso-lin, opposed this further penetration of Japan on the Asian mainland and he had previously expressed his displeasure with the Peking government by calling for the termination of the Sino-Japanese military agreement.[2] Ultimately General Hsü's Mongolian aspirations ruptured the uneasy coalition of the Anfu and Chihli factions in the North, causing prominent Chihli leaders, including General Ts'ao K'un, the military governor of Chihli province, to break with Peking.[3]

Of the great powers, Japan had the least to gain and undoubtedly the most to lose in a struggle between the northern military factions. Tokyo was not only concerned with the fate of the Anfu party but also with that of Chang Tso-lin's Manchuria, the site of heavy Japanese investment since the Sino-Japanese War of 1894-1895. Furthermore, the brewing Anfu-Chihli conflict not only portended damage to Japanese interests in China, but raised the specter of gains for the anti-Japanese government in southern China.

In an attempt to bolster the Peking government during the first half of 1920, Tokyo tried to provide whatever financial aid it could to its sympathizers; for example, throughout the fall and winter of 1919-1920, the four powers attempting to reform the banking Consortium had recognized that the Chinese government desperately needed foreign money to avoid financial catastrophe. But the powers could not agree on the form a loan to that government would take. The Japanese wanted to make an unconditional loan to Peking, whereas the British and Americans feared that such funds would be squandered on military expenses: instead, both Washington and London hoped to ensure that the Chinese could use the proceeds of a loan only for either reproductive purposes or for the disbandment of troops.[4] Tokyo ultimately lost patience with the West's intransigence and moved unilaterally. After accusing Jordan of delaying the loan negotiations, Minister Obata approved a Japanese advance of 9 million yen independent of the other groups in February of 1920. Jordan was outraged:

> There can be no question that we have been out-manoeuvered by Japan in the matter of the loan. As she has now confessed, though she denied it "emphatically" at the time, she has long been committed to provide funds to the present Government. The result has been that after trying to rush us at the last moment and employing the usual methods to throw dust in the eyes of the other Governments, she has done what she always intended to do, namely, made an independent advance and thus established herself as the only foreign Government prepared to help China out of her difficulties.[5]

Jordan did see, however, some advantage resulting from this regrettable incident: "Japan will alone stand the main brunt of the public outburst that will undoubtedly ensue."[6] This bold Japanese action did not solve China's chronic financial distress, and so Tokyo also attempted to alleviate Peking's monetary problems with more subtle maneuvers, such as by arranging a loan via the South Manchurian Railway Company, and by canceling the interest owed to Japan on the remainder of the war participation loan.[7] These measures did not provide a permanent solution, but did allow the Anfu party to concentrate on political problems with the Chihli party and the southern government, rather than on financial affairs.

By the summer of 1920 Tuan and General Hsü Shu-cheng were nearly ready to move against their opponents. On 4 June they announced the mobilization of their forces for an attack against the South. The U. S. chargé d'affaires at Peking reported that the situation in China was critical, and that President Hsü Shih-ch'ang was so discouraged at the state of affairs that he might resign his office.[8] But President Hsü ultimately decided not to submit to the Anfu party. With the support of some of the insurgent northern military governors, and himself affiliated with the Chihli faction, President Hsü even boldly dismissed General Hsü Shu-cheng. The president's insubordination was intolerable to the Anfu leadership; Generals Tuan and Hsü subsequently forced the president to issue mandates disciplining the Chihli leaders, Generals Ts'ao K'un and Wu P'ei-fu. Deciding now to move militarily against his Chihli opponents, on 8 July Tuan placed Peking under martial law without presidential authorization and established an open dictatorship in the capital. Significantly, the Italians were alleged to be supplying Tuan with large amounts of ammunition, while Tuan also tried to prepare British aircraft for use in the imminent conflict.[9]

A crisis was clearly at hand by the second week of July. Washington, London, and Tokyo each faced not merely a test of their commitment to the arms embargo, but of their respective China policies. The question was, how would each country react?

Of the three powers, the United States was the most passive. One possible explanation for Washington's relative inactivity might have been that some policy makers perceived that there was little to gain regardless of which faction prevailed. While no one doubted that Japan's prestige would suffer if the Anfu party was overthrown, the new minister at Peking, Charles Crane, saw little advantage for the United States if the Chihli party triumphed because the issues of popular government and constitutionality in China were not being contested. Crane believed that the struggle was merely one between rival warlords and that the "outlook for [the] formation in the near future of a strong united democratic government appears most discouraging since China has never been more demoralized since [the eighteen-] nineties."[10]

Given the active role of the United States in embargo affairs during the preceding year, one must also ask why neither reports of large Italian arms shipments to Tuan nor rumors of Japanese funding to the Anfu party stirred the State Department during the crisis.[11] Instead Washington focused its attention on the activities of the Diplomatic Corps in Peking, which on 8 July had sent Tuan, President Hsü, and the Wai Chaio Pu a joint note expressing the expectation that no military operations, specifically aerial bombardment, would take place in Peking.[12]   On 16 July Secretary of State Bainbridge Colby questioned the wisdom of such a note, reminding Crane that in 1917 Tuan was not prevented from attacking Chang Hsün's forces within the capital.   Apparently assuming that this prohibition would work to the advantage of Tuan, Colby asked Crane which minister had suggested the joint note, explaining that: "We find it hard to see . . . that the foreign ministers should now deny the liberty of action to those fighting against Tuan which in 1917 they allowed him.   To do so, it seems, would appear to be an act of intervention favoring one party.   To seem to thus take sides might have the direct tendency to arouse hostility against foreigners."[13]   Crane replied five days later (after Chihli forces had routed Tuan's armies) that neither Chinese faction had regarded the ministers' joint note as an act of intervention, explaining that the desire to protect lives and prevent looting had motivated the Diplomatic Corps.[14]

The minister's explanation was still unsatisfactory, and on 23 July Colby curtly requested an answer to his question.   Three days later, Crane admitted that he had authorized a member of the legation to suggest the joint note. Obviously alarmed with Colby's persistence regarding this now moot point, Crane added in defense of his action that "leading Chinese had asked that this be done. We have been thanked informally by the President of China."[15] Finally satisfied, Colby let the matter drop.   Nevertheless, one must ask what accounted for the State Department's preoccupation with the activities of the Diplomatic Corps while apparent violations of the embargo were largely ignored.

Since May 1919, the United States had enforced the China arms embargo under powers granted by Congress to regulate trade during World War I. Secretary of State Robert Lansing realized that the expiration of these war powers would leave Washington unable to uphold the embargo, so he had sought new legislation in the winter and spring of 1919-1920.[16]   By the summer of 1920, however, Congress had shown little inclination to honor Lansing's requests, and as a consequence the State Department no longer believed that it could take the initiative in upholding the embargo.[17] Therefore during the Anfu-Chihli conflict, Colby concerned himself with the ministers' joint note of 8 July, apparently believing that it was either a Japanese maneuver to protect Tuan, or perhaps a British attempt to ensure that their commercial aircraft would not be used in operations over Peking. Ultimately the United States was fortunate in that a more active policy was unnecessary in the summer of 1920.

Unfortunately for London, events did not allow His Majesty's officials the luxury of such a passive a role. Some in the Foreign Office had initially believed that the Anfu-Chihli conflict could benefit both China and Great Britain. While a victory of Tuan's forces might indefinitely postpone a reconciliation between the North and South, the Chihli faction was understood to favor a reconciliation with the South, a reduction of warlord influence, and a less subservient attitude toward Japan.[18]

When informed of the impending crisis, Sir John Jordan took a rather cynical approach not only to the disturbance itself, but to Chinese affairs in general, advising that "there is only one sound policy to pursue and that is to let the Chinese fight it out among themselves, refrain from lending them money, hold up the salt and customs revenues and see that the Powers keep the ring."[19] There was, however, "one small point" which Jordan warned that the Foreign Office should bear in mind; British aircraft in China should not be used for military purposes. Jordan advised that: "We in Peking did not altogether like the whole arrangement and always had a suspicion that in the event of a civil war, the machines might be used for military purposes. . . . The military use of those machines would be a virtual infringement of the agreement about arms, . . . and would expose us to criticism in the South."[20] In the wake of Jordan's warning, the Foreign Office sent an urgent telegram to Peking, emphasizing the "great importance" of preventing Chinese use of British airplanes for military purposes.[21] But in spite of the best efforts of both the British Legation, as well as of Colonel F. V. Holt, the British aviation officer appointed foreign adviser to the Chinese Aeronautical Department, Jordan's fears were realized.

In the week preceding the commencement of hostilities, British pilots in China had made several test flights that had taken them in the vicinity of, and even over, the opposing lines along the Peking-Hankow railway. Great Britain's chargé d'affaires, R. H. Clive, had anticipated that the non-military nature of these flights would probably be misunderstood; therefore two days before Jordan's warning had prompted the Foreign Office's urgent message to Peking, he had requested that British pilots and engineers withdraw from Chinese airdromes.[22] Both Vickers and Handley Page had complied immediately with the Legation's request. Clive informed London that although the Chinese made every effort to use the planes, they could not do so without British assistance.[23] Unfortunately, however, one British airplane "was used on one occasion for bomb dropping by an intoxicated Swiss mechanic who, alone of [the Handley Page] company's employees, ignored [the] written instructions of this Legation."[24] Although Handley Page immediately fired the "intoxicated Swiss mechanic," the damage to British prestige was irreversible, and for the remainder of the year, London was forced to fend off accusations of having violated the arms embargo.[25]

Not only did the military use of a commercial plane keep British diplomats on the defensive, but it also prevented Great Britain from vigorously protesting embargo violations, particularly those of Italian nationals. In March 1920 Rome's chargé d'affaires at Peking, Marquis Durazzo, had had a frank discussion concerning the arms embargo with his British counterpart Miles Lampson. Afterward Lampson reported that the consignments of Italian arms contracted for before 12 May 1919 had all reached China and were stored under Italian supervision. Durazzo also claimed that the Italians had concluded no arms contracts since the imposition of the arms embargo. Lampson added, in a section marked "very confidential":

> [The] Chargé d'Affaires went on to state that he personally was not in sympathy with the attitude adopted by his Government on this question. On his arrival here he had found himself saddled with this disagreeable legacy and had suggested to his Government the advisability of their reconsidering their position but he had received renewed instructions on [the] same lines as his predecessors. He now found himself in a difficult position, having to arrange for the storage of these arms without proper facilities. He was told they were deteriorating and he would be glad to get quit of them and thus wash his hands of these contracts of which he disapproved.[26]

At the end of the month, Durazzo again denied that his government had delivered weapons to the Chinese, although he added that he could not be held accountable for any weapons smuggled into the country.[27] In view of these two emphatic declarations, Lampson believed that Rome had not violated the arms embargo.[28]

Nevertheless the Italian weaponry remained in China and rumors of Italian embargo violations kept surfacing. For example, at the end of May 1920, Rome denied having planned to loan China money to purchase Italian ships and submarines. In spite of the renewed Italian protests of innocence, one Foreign Office official minuted beneath this telegram the comment that "the situation seems far from satisfactory, and it is hard to avoid an uncomfortable suspicion that . . . we are being made fools of by the Japanese and Italians."[29]

This suspicion was well founded. In July the combination of Italian arms and imminent hostilities in China was explosive, and Clive reported:

> As regards the action of the Italians in furnishing General Tuan Ch'i-jui with munitions of war (and it is a fact that they were so furnished), the Italian Minister addressed two letters . . . to the Dean of the Diplomatic Body explaining, and, so far as he was able, excusing the action of his nationals in the matter. In these communications . . . Marquis Durazzo states that the amount of munitions supplied had been greatly exaggerated, that delivery had been made without his knowledge, that he would do his best to prevent further supplies being handed over, and that the material delivered was part of consignments sold under contracts mentioned in the reservations which accompanied Italy's adhesion to the arms embargo arrangement.[30]

Clive hardly needed to add that "Marquis Durazzo's explanations are hardly convincing; and the whole incident has created a deplorable impression in Chinese and foreign circles, and has not enhanced the good name of Italy in this country."[31]

Yet in spite of this flagrant Italian violation of the arms embargo, London could not censure Rome, since the British faced similar charges for having sold China a commercial plane that was used for military purposes. Miles Lampson, now serving with the Foreign Office in London, acknowledged this impediment to British diplomacy when he minuted under Clive's report: "*Note* [emphasis in original] . . . [this incident] in case we want to bombard the Italians again when the Vickers affair is a little clearer."[32] Ultimately, British headaches from the attempt to establish commercial aviation in China led Clive to write that the "whole subject of [the] future of British participation in aviation enterprise in China will have to be reviewed as soon as [the] present internal conflict ends. . . . For [the] moment [the] matter of further purchases from any sources is out of the question."[33]

While the Foreign Office attempted to control the damage to Great Britain's prestige, the Japanese were not immediately concerned either with Peking's military use of British aircraft, or the Italian arms sales, because in both cases these violations of the embargo worked to the advantage of General Tuan. Tokyo did, however, have a real interest in the Anfu-Chihli rupture in the North, and the conflict concerned the Japanese even more once Manchuria's Chang Tso-lin became involved. Chang's disaffection from the Anfu leadership was unexpected, and as Clive reported, "has surprised a good many well-informed people who believed him to be too much under Japanese influence to take up so energetic an attitude in opposition to a faction amongst which the Japanese are supposed to number the few friends they have in China."[34] Tokyo had previously warned Chang against meddling in affairs outside of Manchuria. In 1918 Chang had sent an expedition into central China, which had resulted in a warning from the Japanese consul general at Mukden: "The Three Eastern Provinces are intimately related to Japan. For the man responsible for the maintenance of peace and order there to absent himself unnecessarily from the area and send his army to the center of China is an act likely . . . to interfere with the maintenance of order in the Three Eastern Provinces. . . . I would urge you to refrain from such behavior."[35] Less than two years later, Chang ignored similar warnings against removing his forces from Manchuria,[36] and he again intervened in Chinese affairs, perhaps hoping to replace Tuan's rule for his own.[37]

Chang's insubordination was only one source of Tokyo's discomfort, for there were also large numbers of Japanese officers serving as instructors to Tuan's Frontier Defense Army. Since Tuan was determined to use this force against his Chinese foes, the Japanese minister for foreign affairs sought to head off charges that Japan had intervened in the Chinese civil war; the British ambassador at Tokyo, Sir Charles Eliot, was informed that the "most categorical instructions have been sent to all Japanese officials both military and civil in China and Manchuria to observe strictest neutrality and refrain from encouraging any Chinese faction."[38] Although the Japanese eventually recalled their instructors on 13 July,[39] the Frontier Defense Army was nevertheless still perceived as a Japanese creation, and Tokyo could not avoid implication by proxy in the conflict.

In spite of suspicions regarding the truth of Tokyo's neutrality declarations, the Japanese apparently kept their word, for as one scholar has written, "As the crisis of 1920 developed, there is no evidence of any positive secret initiatives by Japan."[40] In this instance, the Japanese military undoubtedly believed there was no need to intervene. Tuan's soldiers not only had superior weaponry and better training than any other native force, but they were probably unique in being the only Chinese troops not owed their pay.[41] As it happened, Japanese overconfidence was contagious; Anfu generals were so sure of victory that they played mahjong on their train ride to the battlefield.[42]

The rout of the Frontier Defense Army on 18 July was thus completely unexpected. What accounted for the collapse of Tuan's Anfu forces, which was obviously a severe blow to the Japanese? Clive offered one plausible analysis, explaining that "the reason for their rapid demoralization can be ascribed to [the] lack of an ideal for which to fight, and to indecision on the

part of the Anhui [or Anfu] leaders in the conduct of operations."[43]   In
England, Jordan concurred, writing that:

> The news from Peking seems to point to the end of a regime which has been bolstered up and
> kept in power by the Japanese for the last four or five years against the wishes of the people of
> China. I told Count Terauchi in Tokio [sic] in September 1917 that Tuan Ch'i-jui was engaged
> in a losing game and gently hinted that Japan was backing the wrong horse, and the wonder is
> that he has managed to hold on so long.[44]

Although neither diplomat specifically mentioned the arms embargo as a
cause of Tuan's downfall, it nevertheless did materially contribute to the fall
of the pro-Japanese Anfu party. The embargo, as well as the loan ban,
placed a limit on the number of troops that the Anfu party could equip and
fund. Ultimately the size of Tuan's Frontier Defense Army was insufficient
to compensate for its poor morale, which was caused largely by the Anfu
party's close association with Japan. Had the West not been able to impose
the arms embargo and the loan ban, Tuan's army would undoubtedly have
been of sufficient size either to have defeated the Chihli forces, or more
likely, to have inhibited Chihli insubordination in the first place.

From the perspective of both Washington and London, in a little over a
year the China arms embargo had accomplished its primary objective with
the fall of Tuan Ch'i-jui's clique from power. In Tokyo, Hara had gambled
and lost; he had hoped to pursue a cooperative policy with the West while at
the same time maintain the Anfu party in Peking. But Hara's policy failed on
both counts, because the Anfu-Chihli conflict did not allay Western
suspicions of Japan, and Tuan's regime did not survive the test of battle.

The obvious question facing the powers in the summer of 1920 was what
to do with the embargo. Although some in the United States and Great
Britain called for the termination of the agreement, they did not do so on the
grounds that the policy had succeeded and was therefore no longer necessary.
Rather, those attacking the embargo claimed that it had not prevented arms
from reaching China, and that Washington and London therefore penalized
home armament industries to the benefit of those foreign manufacturers
whose governments did not enforce or recognize the agreement.

But for several reasons neither the United States nor Great Britain
seriously entertained proposals for ending the embargo. First of all, in May
of 1919 the embargoing powers had publicly committed themselves to uphold
the agreement pending an end to the civil war and the reestablishment of a
unified government in China. Tuan's defeat represented the demise of only

one of several Chinese factions, and the conflict between the North and South continued unabated. Thus the Chinese were no closer to ending their civil war after the Anfu-Chihli conflict.

Furthermore there were diplomatic motives involved in the maintenance of the embargo; most importantly it would have embarrassed Tokyo to terminate the agreement immediately upon Tuan's defeat. This would have openly implied that the Anfu warlords, and by extension Japan, were the embargo's targets. Although this was true, such a gratuitous insult to the principal Far Eastern power could not be considered sound policy by even ardently anti-Japanese officials.

Finally it would have also not made good business sense to remove the embargo in the summer of 1920. Certainly the embargo did not benefit arms manufacturers, who represented an important and influential sector of the British and American economies. However, the continuation of the Chinese civil war posed an even greater threat not only to foreign-owned enterprises within China, but also to the larger export and financial sectors in the United States and Great Britain. Thus the arms embargo was maintained in order to restore prosperity, as well as peace, to China. Unfortunately a combination of factors not fully appreciated in May 1919 would continue to frustrate the hope that the embargo would force a swift conclusion to hostilities.

NOTES

1. Jordan to Curzon, 1 March 1920, Annual Report for 1919, F.O. 405/229, 182053, PRO.

2. Crane to Colby, 16 December 1920, 893.00/3731, FRUS 1920, p. 436.

3. Crane to Colby, 10 July 1920, 893.00/3385, FRUS 1920, pp. 439-40.

4. See Jordan to Curzon, 18 and 21 February 1920, F 472/2/10 and F 567/2/10, DBFP, 1st ser., vol. 6, pp. 998-1001, 1006-8.

5. Jordan to Curzon, 21 February 1920, F 472/2/10, DBFP, 1st ser., vol. 6, p. 1007.

6. Ibid.

7. John Young, p. 135.

8. Tenney to Colby, 4 June 1920, 893.3365, DSNA. For a paraphrase, see FRUS 1920, p. 423.

9. See Crane to Colby, 8-10 July 1920, 893.00/3379, 893.00/3380, and 893.00/3385, all in FRUS 1920, pp. 437-40.

10. Crane to Colby, 10 July 1920, 893.00/3385, FRUS 1920, p. 440.

11. Crane to Colby, 9 July 1920, 893.00/3880, FRUS 1920, p. 438.

12. Ibid.

13. Colby to Crane, 16 July 1920, 893.00/3380, FRUS 1920, p. 443. The next day Colby reinforced his point by asking that the substance of his 16 July telegram be repeated to the United States consul at Tientsin "so that he will not participate inadvertently in any action . . . which might actually or colorably constitute an intervention on behalf of any of the factions involved in the present struggle." Colby to Crane, 17 July 1920, 893.00/3393, FRUS 1920, pp. 445-46.

14. Crane to Colby, 21 July 1920, 893.00/3409, FRUS 1920, p. 453.

15. Colby to Crane, 23 July 1920, 893.00/3409; Crane to Colby, 26 July 1920, 893.00/3419, FRUS 1920, pp. 454-55.

16. See Lansing to Senator Gilbert Hitchcock, 31 December 1919, 693.119/298a; and Lansing to Senator Henry Cabot Lodge, Jr., 16 March 1920, 693.119/309, DSNA.

17. Colby to Crane, 24 September 1920, 693.119/352, FRUS 1920, p. 750.

18. Memo of C. Campbell, 23 July 1920, F.O. 371/5338, F 1549/865/10, PRO. However, by the fall of 1920, the British realized that the Anfu-Chihli conflict had only served to substitute one set of military leaders for another. See the minute by Miles Lampson under Clive to Curzon, 13 September 1920, F.O. 371/5339, F 2645/865/10, PRO. Lampson added, "The only real hope is that the slowly awakening *national* [emphasis in original] sentiment may at last become articulate and insist upon some real voice in the country's government. Possibly Japanese aggression may in this respect achieve the otherwise apparently impossible."

19. Minute by Victor Wellesley under Clive to Curzon, 11 July 1920, F.O. 371/5338, F 1427/865/10, PRO.

20. Jordan to Wellesley, 14 July 1920, F.O. 371/5338, F 1472/865/10, PRO.

21. Hardinge to Clive, 14 July 1920, F 1472/865/10, DBFP, 1st ser., vol. 14, p. 72.

22. Clive to Curzon, 21 July 1920, F.O. 405/228, F 2415/865/10, PRO.

23. Clive to Curzon, 13 July 1920, F 1479/865/10, DBFP, 1st ser., vol. 14, pp. 71-72.

24. Alston to Curzon, 14 December 1920, F 3240/1/10, DBFP, 1st ser., vol. 14, pp. 196-97. See also Clive to Curzon, 21 July 1920, F.O. 405/228, F 2415/865/10, PRO.

25. Alston to Curzon, 14 December 1920, F 3240/1/10, DBFP., 1st ser., vol. 14, pp. 196-97. See also note 2 on p. 196.

26. Lampson to Curzon, 16 March 1920, F 303/1/10, DBFP, 1st ser., vol. 6, p. 1041.

27. Lampson to Curzon, 29 March 1920, F.O. 371/5295, F 341/1/10, PRO.

28. Lampson to Curzon, 13 April 1920, F.O. 371/5296, F 1301/1/10, PRO. Lampson believed Durazzo's declarations, stating: "It would obviously be in the highest degree foolish for him to make such categorical statements if untrue, as the facts would most certainly come out eventually in China where nothing remains unknown for long."

29. Hubbard minute under Buchanan to Curzon, 29 May 1920, F.O. 371/5295, F 1048/1/10, PRO.

30. Clive to Curzon, 23 July 1920, F.O. 371/5339, F 2461/865/10, PRO.

31. Ibid.

32. Minute by Lampson under Clive to Curzon, 23 July 1920, F.O. 371/5339, F 2461/865/10, PRO.

33. Clive to Curzon, 20 July 1920, F.O. 371/ 5296, F 1612/1/10, PRO.

34. Clive to Curzon, 30 July 1920, F.O. 371/5339, F 2424/865/10, PRO.

35. Quoted in McCormack, p. 49.

36. On 11 July Clive informed London that "I learn on good authority that a warning has been conveyed to the latter [Chang Tso-lin] by the Japanese that it will be well for him not to remove any of his forces from Manchuria, as in the event of his doing so it would be necessary for Japan, for the sake of her troops who are on the point of withdrawing from Trans-Barkalia, to interfere in Manchurian affairs more closely than she has done in the past." Clive to Curzon, 11 July 1920, F.O. 371/5339, F 2414/865/10, PRO. That same day Clive sent another message to London concerning Chang Tso-lin: "From statements made by [the] Japanese Military Attaché and by [the] Japanese owner of [a] vernacular organ it is safe to infer that [the] Military Governor of Mukden has been neutralized by hints of trouble in Manchuria." See Clive to Curzon, 11 July 1920, F.O. 371/5338, F 1454/865/10 PRO.

37. McCormack, p. 49.

38. Eliot to Curzon, 12 July 1920, F.O. 371/5338, F 1458/865/10, PRO.

39. Crane to Colby, 13 July 1920, 693.119/334, FRUS 20, pp. 440-41. While on the one hand the Japanese did withdraw their instructors, on the other hand both the army minister and the foreign minister agreed that Tokyo should do nothing to prevent the Frontier Defense Army's use in the

civil war. McCormack, p. 51.

40. McCormack, p. 50. Washington did recognize the peculiar handicaps under which the civilian Japanese government labored. In March 1920 Secretary of the Navy Josephus Daniels forwarded a report to the State Department from the commander-in-chief of the Asiatic fleet, which read in part: "Japan is essentially a military nation; monarchistic in ideas and methods. The Military Party is in actual control of the government. Statements and explanations made by the Premier and the Foreign Office may be made in good faith, but the Military Party carries out its policy without regard to the other branches of Government." Daniels to the Secretary of State, 9 March 1920, 893.00/3314, DSNA. It is interesting to note that the report also contained the opinion that "Japan is a young nation that has achieved so much superficial success that it has gone to her head. No remedy will come except through a hard knock or fall."

41. Denny to Bentinck, 27 July 1920, F.O. 371/5338, F 1627/865/10, PRO. See also McCormack, pp. 51-52.

42. Chi, "Ts'ao Ju-lin: His Japanese Connection," in Iriye, *The Chinese and Japanese,* p. 151.

43. Clive to Curzon, 26 July 1920, F.O. 371/5339, F 2422/865/10, PRO. Japanese prestige sank even lower in China when fugitive Anfu leaders sought, and received, sanctuary within the Japanese Legation.

44. Jordan to Bentinck, 27 July 1920, F.O. 371/5338, F 1650/865/10, PRO. Minister Crane gave Washington a similar assessment: "At first gains [were] reported for the Anfuites, but it soon became apparent that the troops of General Wu [P'ei-fu] though less well equipped than those of the opposition, who possessed liberal quantities of arms and ammunition, some of Japanese and Italian origin, had greater efficiency in action and morale and in addition more aggressive leadership. Under Tuan were the two mixed brigades of the Frontier Defense Force, totalling about 30,000 and in addition the 9th, 13th, and 15th divisions, the loyalty of the latter being doubtful. . . . Lacking effective leadership in the field, with a broken down commissariat, and *with little stomach for fighting for their pro-Japanese superiors* [emphasis added], the Anfu troops were rapidly withdrawn toward Peking." Crane to Colby, 26 January 1921, 893.00/3787, FRUS 1920, p. 465.

7

Britain Defends
the Embargo

By the fall of 1920 Great Britain had become the arms embargo's principal defender. In the wake of the Anfu-Chihli war, the British Legation at Peking still considered China to be in a "chaotic" state, and the central government's financial position as "deplorable" as ever. Both Chargé d'Affaires Clive and the Foreign Office agreed that for the Chinese to buy arms was a "sheer waste of money" and that "such transactions were bound to foster civil war and internal dissension in the country."[1]

London gradually discovered, however, that the other powers did not necessarily share the desire to maintain the embargo. During a conversation with Italian Minister Marquis Durazzo, Clive received the distinct impression that Rome sanctioned the contracting of arms for delivery upon the embargo's termination. Ominously, Durazzo implied that the French were concluding similar arrangements. Indeed France was on the verge of assuming a less constructive attitude toward the embargo. The Vickers contract had especially miffed the French, and in January 1921 the French air attaché at Peking even proposed to Minister Charles Crane a plan of Franco-American cooperation against British aviation in China.[2]

Even more worrisome to the British, however, was a new American attitude toward the embargo. On 8 September 1920 Crane, in view of the sale of British commercial aircraft to China, asked if the State Department would permit similar American sales.[3] Colby replied in the middle of the month that, while the State Department had been inclined to place as broad an interpretation on the embargo as possible, since "other Governments have permitted their nationals to enter into contracts for commercial airplanes, this Government does not feel warranted in interposing objections to its nationals doing likewise in case the airplanes are designed and built strictly for commercial use."[4] Clearly, Washington would have preferred not to relax the arms embargo; nevertheless the State Department was forced to change its stance because it could not answer satisfactorily inquiries into British airplane sales from American manufacturers (such as the Curtiss Aeroplane & Motor Company) excluded from the China market.

The United States was not ready, however, to go so far as to terminate the embargo. It was true that some American officials, especially the acting commercial attaché at Peking Charles C. Batchelder, had denounced the embargo as "totally ineffective" and believed that its only visible effect had been to cause American businessmen to lose many profitable sales. Batchelder informed his superiors that the embargo was "a dead letter except as regards Americans" and referred to the July fighting in China, as well as the numerous alleged embargo violations, to support his opinion.[5]

Colby returned Batchelder's report to Peking in order to solicit the opinion of the American minister. Crane acknowledged that there had been violations of the embargo, but he believed that: "At [the] present moment [the] claim that American companies are discriminated against and that [the] embargo on arms to China is a dead letter is much exaggerated."[6] Spurred on by Batchelder's remarks, Crane proposed to his colleagues that the United States, Great Britain, France, and Japan make a new declaration in support of the embargo. Their resulting joint note, after expressing apprehension concerning past Italian violations, asked each power to reiterate its adherence to the embargo, and also offered a "pressing invitation" to Rome to renew formally the assurances made in May 1919.[7]

Surprisingly, Colby reproached Crane for his initiative: "It is the opinion of the Department that [a] reiteration of the arms embargo agreement will serve no useful purpose and also that it would not be opportune for the United States to take any initiative in the matter at this time in view of the fact that the embargo can be enforced in the United States only by virtue of war powers which probably will soon be terminated."[8] Colby explained that he had not forwarded Batchelder's report to Peking in order to initiate new action, but rather to garner information on the effectiveness of the embargo, so that the administration could decide whether or not to ask Congress for a special grant of power to enforce the agreement. Colby did not, however, repudiate the ministers' joint note; instead he told Crane to take no further action beyond reporting the replies of the other powers.[9]

With the United States sending out mixed signals, on the one hand apparently asking for a reaffirmation of the embargo, while on the other hand relaxing its interpretation of the agreement to permit the sale of commercial aircraft, the British received even worse news. On 9 October Clive informed London that Chang Tso-lin had acquired some of the Peking government's British-made planes, and planned to take them back to Manchuria as war booty. Given Chang's openly avowed intention to use the machines for military purposes, London was obviously placed in an embarrassing position vis-à-vis the other embargo powers.[10]

Although the powerless Peking government could not compel Chang to return the aircraft, the incident ultimately did not harm London. Chang could not use the planes because he had no trained pilots to fly them; he had none of the Castrol oil necessary for the engines; and in any case, careless packing had rendered most of the planes useless for flying.[11] Nevertheless the possibility that a similar situation in the future might not work out as fortunately further reinforced the Foreign Office's determination to avoid the mistake of selling more commercial airplanes to China.

London was also concerned by Tokyo's attitude toward the embargo after the Anfu-Chihli war. Tuan's fall had obviously necessitated a reassessment of Japan's China policy. If Tokyo wanted to continue to influence Chinese affairs to the extent it had during Tuan's time, the Japanese had to find a new Chinese client. In this regard, Chang Tso-lin was not only the leading candidate, but he actively attempted to represent himself as a new Tuan Ch'i-jui, deserving of at least as much Japanese support and aid as Tuan.[12]

With the particular backing of senior Kwantung Army officers and most of Japan's military establishment in China, Chang had indeed succeeded Tuan as Japan's favored client by the fall of 1920. But Tokyo still had to decide the extent to which Chang should receive Japanese support. Crucial in making this decision was the determination of whether Chang was perceived to be only a pro-Japanese official confined to Manchuria, or a prospective unifier of the country.[13]

The Hara cabinet deliberated for the better part of a year concerning the amount of support to be given Chang. After consulting the civil and military officials of the departments concerned with Chinese affairs at the Eastern Conference in May 1921, Tokyo decided that "in general the [Japanese] empire should offer Chang Tso-lin aid both direct and indirect in reorganizing and developing the civil affairs and military preparedness of the Three Eastern Provinces and in establishing his firm authority over the region." Significantly, Tokyo would not aid Chang if he sought assistance "in order to accomplish his ambition in central political affairs."[14] Thus Tokyo decided to leash Chang in Manchuria, providing him with only enough aid to protect Japanese interests.

The Hara government decided that in order to avoid suspicion, Japan would grant financial support to Chang in the form of loans, especially those to promote joint Sino-Japanese enterprises.[15] In addition, Tokyo instructed that the letter of the arms embargo should be observed, and Chang should not receive direct supplies of arms from Japan. However, the Hara government left open the possibility to circumvent the agreement by assisting Chang to build an arsenal, which would help him become self-sufficient in weapons.[16]

The Japanese minister at Peking indicated Tokyo's attitude toward the embargo itself in the fall of 1920. During the 23 September meeting of the Diplomatic Corps at which Crane suggested that the powers ask Italy to renew its pledge to uphold the embargo, the Japanese minister had insisted on adding the declaration that "failing such assurances, it is to be feared that [the] other governments may feel justified in resuming their liberty of action."[17] The Japanese did not immediately move to carry out their threat by making arms shipments to China, but the Foreign Office was nevertheless alarmed at the prospect of an end to the embargo.[18] For nearly the next three months Tokyo manifested displeasure with the embargo by delaying a joint protest in Rome with the British and French, which led Lampson to despair the embargo's future by early December: "Both the Japanese and the Italians ask nothing better than to scrap the embargo on arms. And if, as seems possible, matters work up to that, it is primarily *we* [emphasis in original] who shall be responsible. The Vickers aeroplane contract will be the peg upon which action will be hung. It was a wicked proceeding and we are now reaping the whirlwind."[19] Lampson's warnings were prescient. On 8 December 1920 the Japanese finally attacked the embargo, proposing a new agreement which, in light of the various embargo violations, would permit the completion of contracts made before May 1919.[20]

Both the Legation at Peking and the Foreign Office opposed the Japanese plan. Minister Alston informed London that the "present state of relations between North and South, far from being an argument in the interest of [a] relaxation of [the] embargo, offers [the] strongest grounds for reaffirmation."[21] Officials within the Foreign Office used even more pointed language: "Agreement with the Japanese proposal would stultify, and render absolutely nugatory our whole policy re: the arms embargo in China. . . . In the interests of restoring peace in China, we should turn down absolutely this Japanese proposal, which is another instance of their slipperiness."[22] How could the British save the embargo given the apparently apathetic, if not hostile, attitude of the other powers?

Curzon moved first in Rome, since in spite of their differences, the powers could at least agree that Italy's evasions of the embargo were a major problem.[23] Referring to the embargo as "without doubt the proper policy to pursue," Curzon blamed Rome's failure to enforce the agreement for causing the vacillating attitude toward the embargo of several other governments. Attempting to preempt Italian countercharges concerning British embargo violations, he also instructed Sir George Buchanan at Rome to avoid alluding to the Vickers contract; if the Italians brought up this case, Buchanan was to argue that the improper use of British aircraft "in no way constitutes an evasion" of the embargo.[24] Rome answered London's representation with the familiar statement that if Italian arms were supplied to Chinese purchasers, it was done in execution of pre-May 1919 contracts. Although the Italian reply was "entirely unsatisfactory," London's action in Rome allowed the British to regain some credibility as a defender of the embargo.[25]

Curzon sent Sir Charles Eliot in Tokyo instructions similar to those he had sent to Buchanan in Rome. If anything, Curzon chose harsher words for Japan, pointing out that recently the Japanese had displayed a "disposition to harp on [the] Vickers contract and to seek in it a breach of the embargo."[26] Curzon emphatically repudiated this insinuation and cited London's actions during the Anfu-Chihli war to defend Britain's integrity. Surprisingly, Minister Uchida agreed with the British position on the Vickers aircraft, but expressed concern about a recently contemplated Handley Page contract.[27] Although Uchida was not satisfied with Eliot's explanation that the British Legation at Peking refused to have anything to do with that particular contract, he did eventually admit that the moment was not opportune to relax the arms embargo.[28]

Curzon, still not pleased with Tokyo's attitude, instructed Eliot to "leave his Excellency in no doubt that any departure by Japan from [the] embargo policy will be viewed by His Majesty's Government as tending to prolong [the] disturbed state of China and as an aggravation of the situation."[29] In spite of the British warning, the Japanese refused to drop their desire to relax the embargo, and only conceded that they were in no hurry to press the issue. Ultimately, however, the British realized the substance of victory as the Japanese did not renew their proposal.[30]

Ironically, Washington gave London more trouble over the embargo than
did Tokyo. By mid-January 1921, Alston warned London that Washington
was "very luke-warm on the subject of [the] embargo."[31] On 10 January the
U.S. ambassador at London was more specific; the American government
might soon lose the power to enforce the embargo, and the "information thus
far available scarcely warrants such a confidence in the practical efficacy of
the embargo as would justify a request being submitted to Congress for a
continuance of the special powers by which restrictions have up to the
present, been imposed upon American manufacturers."[32] Within the Foreign
Office Miles Lampson found a more direct reason for the American attitude:
"It is all the result of the cursed Vickers contract which confronts us (and
rightly so) at every turn. We have sown the wind and are now reaping the
whirl-wind."[33] How could London convince Washington of Britain's wish to
maintain the embargo, given that the Vickers deal was an accomplished fact?

Over the next six weeks, British diplomats subjected their American
counterparts to many hours of patient diplomacy. Victor Wellesley, head of
the Far Eastern Department at the Foreign Office, revealed a central feature
of London's major concession to the United States with the statement that:
"We recognize in the light of subsequent events that the [Vickers] transaction
had been a mistake and no one deplored it more than we did. . . . We were
prepared to rule out aeroplanes definitely for the future but . . . we could not
make any such ruling retrospective as regards the Vickers contract in view of
the loan which had been floated in this country."[34] Actually, Wellesley
conceded very little to the United States, because London had decided to
prohibit further sales of aircraft to China.[35]

London's strategy succeeded. On 26 February 1921 the British
ambassador at Washington informed London that the "U.S Government are
firmly convinced of the great importance of maintaining the embargo."[36] The
State Department also noted that legislation would soon be introduced in
Congress to allow the United States government to continue to enforce the
agreement. But Washington did warn the British that opposition in
Congress, largely stimulated by embargo violations of other powers, could
block the passage of any such legislation.

Needless to say, the Foreign Office was pleased with this evidence that
the United States had adopted a "more reasonable" attitude toward the
embargo. London had single-handedly persuaded both Washington and
Tokyo to maintain the China arms embargo. Unfortunately for the British,
they could not yet put down the burden of being the embargo's principal

champion.

Less than one week after Washington reaffirmed its commitment to the arms embargo, a congressional joint resolution repealed those sections of the Espionage Act under which the United States had controlled arms shipments to China.[37] The new administration of President Warren G. Harding responded quickly to the situation in a manner that fully satisfied London.[38] On 14 March the new secretary of state, Charles Evans Hughes, wrote to Henry Cabot Lodge, Jr., the chairman of the Senate Committee on Foreign Relations, requesting legislation "to enable this Government to continue its cooperation with the other Powers in a policy which it believes necessary under existing circumstances."[39] In addition, Hughes informed each of the other embargoing powers that, in spite of Congress' action, the United States had not changed its policy and would still refuse to support any American effort to sell arms to China.[40]

Congress, however, moved slowly in honoring Hughes' request, and so between 3 March 1921 and 4 March 1922, the U.S. government did not have the power to compel its citizens to refrain from selling arms to China. While such transactions could not be legally prevented, State Department officials did whatever they could to discourage firms inquiring about the China market for war materials. For example, on 27 May 1921 Assistant Secretary of State F. M. Dearing wrote to H. A. Astlett & Co. of New York that "under the circumstances, the policy of this Government is opposed to the shipment of any material of the kind [rifles and one-inch-bore field cannons] mentioned in your letter to China at the present time."[41] Dearing's letter to the company was misleading; although as a matter of policy the U.S. government opposed the shipment of arms to China, he failed to point out that the U.S. government could not legally prevent such a trade.

Delay was another favorite ploy of the State Department. In June the director of DuPont's military sales department forwarded a letter to Secretary Hughes from the company's agent in China, which stated that large quantities of rifle powder could be sold in that country, and he inquired about the possibility of the embargo's removal in the near future. Since the department did not favor the company with an immediate response, DuPont sent a second letter to Washington in July. Finally in August Hughes gave the following verbose reply:

The Department regrets the delay in replying to your two letters and can only say at this time that the matter concerning which you inquire has been under exhaustive examination. The Department is not in a position to give a ["definite" stricken out] reply to your inquiries at this time because of certain phases of the question which have a bearing on the relations between this and other governments. It will be necessary, therefore, for the Department to defer action on your request until certain information which it is now seeking has been obtained."[42]

There is no evidence in the State Department's files indicating that DuPont pursued this matter further. On the whole, then, the State Department's tactics succeeded in preventing large shipments of arms to China from the United States.

Almost inevitably, however, some American war material did reach China. One of the most prominent cases concerned the cargo ship *Wondrichen*, which delivered equipment to the Canton arsenal. While the shipment had cleared U.S. customs at a time when the government could still enforce the embargo, officials had had "no indication that the machinery was for other than commercial purposes,"[43] and once that was discovered, American authorities could not prevent delivery.

The lack of authority to enforce the embargo did not necessitate any drastic change in American diplomacy. Initially, however, Hughes and the department were reluctant to take any action concerning the embargo, even in conjunction with other powers. For example, on 14 March 1921 London requested that the American ambassador at Tokyo join with his British colleague to prevent the Japanese from trying to relax the embargo.[44] In April Washington politely declined the British invitation, expressing the desire to await fresh legislation from Congress.[45]

By the end of the year, however, Washington did react, along with the other powers, to flagrant Italian embargo violations. On 3 September Consul Douglas Jenkins at Harbin notified Minister Jacob Gould Schurman that the Italians were again selling arms, apparently with the full support of the legation at Peking. The next month Jenkins added that the new Italian consul had just arrested his own brother, who until recently had been a consular agent, and charged him with trafficking in arms and opium.[46] In keeping with its low profile on the embargo while Congress deliberated new legislation, the State Department took no action until Schurman reported on 9 December that the

Japanese Minister having ascertained that arms which had been stored in [the] Italian barracks at Shanhaikwan were being handed over to [the] Military Governor of Chihli inquired of [the] Italian Chargé d'Affaires who tried to justify [the] sale on the ground [that the] embargo agreement had not been recognized by his Government in respect of arms contracted for before its adoption. He considers himself at liberty to dispose of [the] arms until he receives orders to the contrary. It is noteworthy that arms were handed over secretly at [on] nights of

November 21st and 22nd. It was ascertained [the] quantity delivered was 80 wagon loads.[47]

Schurman and his British, French, and Japanese colleagues recommended that the matter be brought to the attention of the Conference on the Limitation of Armaments at Washington. In addition, Hughes, after a request by Tokyo, authorized Ambassador Richard Child at Rome separately but simultaneously to join his colleagues in making a protest to the Italian government.[48]

For the Italians, then, the faux pas of the November arms sales not only invited renewed diplomatic criticism from the powers, but from the delegations attending the Washington Conference as well. Rome responded to the diplomatic attack with the tried and true tactics of denial and delay. On 30 January 1922 Child transmitted Italy's reply, repeating its reservation of the right to complete arms contracts concluded before May 1919. Adding a new twist, Rome also noted that the recent arms deliveries were made only after the government of Chihli province made formal assurances "to the effect that the material would be kept in magazines and would not be used in any manner in the internal wars of China."[49] As always, the Italian explanation was not satisfactory, because both Washington and London considered the pledges of Chinese warlords worthless.

Meanwhile the delegates to the Washington Conference had attempted to strengthen the embargo by drafting a resolution asking signatory powers "to refrain from exporting to China arms or munitions of war, whether complete or in parts."[50] Although the Italian delegation "were entirely in favor of the Resolution," they never received authorization to adopt it, allegedly because Rome was unsure whether or not the government could enforce its provisions. In the face of Italian procrastination, the resolution was withdrawn.[51]

Italy's persistent opposition to both the spirit and letter of the embargo were not, however, forgotten in Washington, especially after Congress passed a joint resolution on 31 January 1922 declaring:

That whenever the President finds that in any American country, or in any country in which the United States exercises extraterritorial jurisdiction, conditions of domestic violence exist, which are or may be promoted by the use of arms or munitions of war procured from the United States, and makes proclamation thereof, it shall be unlawful to export, except under such limitations and exceptions as the President prescribes, any arms or munitions of war from any place in the United States to such country until otherwise ordered by the President or by Congress.[52]

On 4 March, by virtue of the authority conferred by Congress, Harding applied the resolution to China. That same day Acting Secretary of State Henry P. Fletcher instructed Child to ask the Italian government to abandon its reservation to the arms declaration of May 1919 "in view of the disastrous effect which the maintenance of such a reservation and the consequent further delivery of munitions to contending factions in China may have."[53] On 13 April the beleaguered Italians finally directed the legation at Peking to make no further arms deliveries to the Chinese.[54]

After nearly three years of effort, the powers with representatives at Peking in May 1919 had finally accepted the China arms embargo without reservation. The agreement had survived warfare, violation, and indifference, apparently to become fully effective in the spring of 1922. Unfortunately this expression of international cooperation was only illusory.

Even as the Italians moved toward accepting the embargo, many signs indicated that both old and new factors would conspire to undermine the agreement. For their part, Japanese military leaders, piqued by what they considered the meager aid that the civilian government permitted Chang Tso-lin, moved to provide him with military support. Furthermore, by the summer of 1922 the Italians were again uncooperative. In July Rome declined to adopt the China arms embargo resolution negotiated at the Washington Conference because of a ministerial crisis. By September Italy refused to adhere formally to this resolution in view of its previous declarations in support of the embargo and pending a meeting of the Diplomatic Corps in Peking on the subject. Rome, while not renouncing the embargo itself, thus refused to support the principle of international cooperation necessary for the success of such an undertaking.[55]

Several developments since 1919 also threatened the integrity of the embargo. By 1922 the Germans, previously in no position to sell war material to China, were able to do so along with citizens of countries that had not existed in May 1919 (such as Czechoslovakia). While these sales were undertaken for financial rather than political gain, they provided ammunition for those desiring the embargo's termination. The activities of the Soviet Union were even more ominous. In the years immediately following the 1917 revolution, Vladimir Ilich Lenin had presided over a divided and war-torn country. However, by 1922, increasingly sure of their position at home and seeking to expand influence abroad, the Soviets flouted the embargo and intervened in the Chinese civil war in search of political advantage.

NOTES

1. Clive to Curzon, 20 September 1920, F.O. 405/225, F 3019/1/10, PRO.

2. Ibid. See also Crane to Colby, 4 January 1921, 893.113/104, DSNA.

3. Crane to Colby, 8 September 1920, 693.119/346, FRUS 1920, p. 746.

4. Colby to Crane, 17 September 1920, 693.119/346, FRUS 1920, p. 748.

5. Charles C. Batchelder to the Department of Commerce, 23 July 1920, enclosed in Eldridge to Lockhart, 10 September 1920, 693.119/351, FRUS 1920, pp. 747-48.

6. Crane to Colby, 23 September 1920, 693.119/352, FRUS 1920, p. 749.

7. Crane to Colby, 23 September 1920, 693.119/353, FRUS 1920, pp. 749-50.

8. Colby to Crane, 24 September 1920, 693.119/352, FRUS 1920, p. 750.

9. Colby to Crane, 1 October 1920, 693.119/353, FRUS 1920, p. 750.

10. See Clive to Curzon, 9 October 1920, F 2348/1/10, DBFP, 1st ser., vol. 14, p. 151. Sir John Jordan commented in a private letter: "I see Chang Tso-lin has collared the Handley Page and Vickers aeroplanes. I don't suppose you are at all surprised--the whole thing was a mistake from the outset, as we always thought. Let us hope that this experience will be a lesson to people who foist useless and expensive toys upon China, and impair the value of the country as an asset for genuine trade. Equipping China with aviation material for commercial purposes is all moonshine in present circumstances." 15 October 1920, F.O. 371/5296, F 2807/1/10, PRO.

11. Curzon to Clive, 19 October 1920, F 2348/1/10, DBFP, 1st ser., vol. 14, p. 158. Clive to Curzon, 24 November 1920, F 2936/1/10, DBFP, 1st ser., vol. 14, pp. 182-83.

12. McCormack, p. 56.

13. Ibid., p. 57.

14. Ibid., p. 58.

15. On page 59, McCormack provides the following translation of the position of the government regarding financial aid: "While the imperial government is not unwilling to give friendly consideration to financial aid according to circumstances, it is important to do so by means of economic loans, especially by adopting the form of investment in joint enterprises, in order to avoid the suspicion of the powers and the jealousy of the central government. If Chang Tso-lin too will strive increasingly to promote the reality of Sino-Japanese cooperation, exerting himself, for example, in

relation to the lease of land, the management of mines and forests, and other such promising enterprises, and if he will apply every effort to implementing the principle of so-called coexistence and coprosperity and devise methods of joint control both in already existing and in newly to be set up Sino-Japanese joint venture companies, then the finances of the Three Eastern Provinces can be made to flourish of their own accord and in an inconspicuous way."

16. Ibid., pp. 58-59.

17. See Crane to Colby, 23 September and 4 December 1920, 693.119/353, 693.119/378, FRUS 1920, pp. 749-52.

18. Within the Foreign Office, B. C. Newton minuted that "I should doubt whether we should be well-advised to threaten . . . the resumption of our liberty of action, especially as it would be most unfortunate if this threat were carried out." See the minutes under Clive to Curzon 23 September 1920, F.O. 371/5296, F 2209/1/10, PRO. Two months later, Miles Lampson was of the opinion that "it is quite evident from what Mr. Clive says, that the Japanese are anxious to find an opportunity of annulling the embargo, [and] I think it is essential we should do all in our power to strengthen it as soon as possible." Lampson minute under Clive to Curzon, 24 November 1920, F.O. 371/5296, F 2933/1/10, PRO.

19. Lampson minute under Buchanan to Curzon, 5 December 1920, F.O. 371/5297, F 3092/1/10, PRO.

20. Eliot to Curzon, 8 December 1920, F.O. 371/5297, F 3173/1/10, PRO.

21. Alston to Curzon, 14 December 1920, F 3240/1/10, DBFP, 1st ser., vol. 14, pp. 196-97. To make matters worse for London, that same day Alston reported that Handley Page had signed an agreement with the Chinese government for the sale of 105 flying boats and hydroplanes at a cost of £897,200 and for an additional credit of £400,000. Alston was enraged because the company's agent had deliberately concealed negotiations of this agreement from the legation and he believed that "viewed in light of: (a) Present impasse regarding existing aviation contracts.   (b) Arms embargo. (c) Consortium. (d) Good name of British enterprises in this country and of Chinese securities in Great Britain (payment of interest of Messrs. Vickers' loan, contracted only a year ago, is still in arrears, and likely to remain so): conclusion of this agreement at present juncture can only be described as disastrous." Alston to Curzon, 14 December 1920, F 3226/1/10, DBFP, 1st ser., vol. 14, pp. 198-99. See also note 35 below.

22. Minute by A. E. Easter under Eliot to Curzon, 8 December 1920, F. O. 371/5297, F 3173/1/10, PRO. In summarizing the British position,

Lampson wrote that "the already existing chaos in China would be aggravated a hundredfold if there were unrestricted freedom of import of arms and ammunition from abroad." See 18 December 1920, F.O. 371/5297, F 3279/1/10, PRO.

23. The Foreign Office was incredulous upon learning that the Japanese ambassador at Rome had joined his colleagues in protesting Italian lukewarmness towards the arms embargo, while at the same time Tokyo proposed to circumvent the embargo with respect to its own unfulfilled contracts. London, however, considered the Japanese verbal communication to Rome inadequate, given that the United States, Great Britain, and France had presented written notes. Lampson could only surmise that "it is possible that whilst joining in the representations at Rome the Japanese Government still mean *eventually* [emphasis in original] to bring the whole question up again." See the minutes under Buchanan to Curzon, 18 December 1920, F.O. 371/5297, F 3279/1/10, PRO, and Curzon to Eliot, 6 January 1921, F 5/2/10, DBFP, 1st ser., vol. 14, p. 204.

24. Curzon to Buchanan, 14 December 1920, F.O. 405/228, F 3019/1/10, PRO.

25. Buchanan to Curzon, 2 February 1921, F.O. 405/230, F 400/2/10, PRO.

26. Curzon to Eliot, 3 January 1921, F 3279/1/10, DBFP, 1st ser., vol. 14, pp. 202-3.

27. See note 21.

28. Eliot to Curzon, 9 January 1921, F 141/2/10, DBFP, 1st ser., vol. 14, p. 205.

29. Curzon to Eliot, 14 January 1921, F 120/2/10, DBFP, 1st ser., vol. 14, p. 213.

30. See Eliot to Curzon, 16 and 27 January 1921, F 205/2/10 and F 346/2/10, DBFP, 1st ser., vol. 14, pp. 214, 231.

31. Alston to Curzon, 16 January 1921, F.O. 405/230, F 188/2/10, PRO.

32. Davis to Curzon, 12 January 1921, F.O. 405/230, F 120/2/10, PRO. See also the Acting Secretary of State to Davis, 7 January 1921, 693.119/379, FRUS 1921, p. 536.

33. Lampson minute under Davis to Curzon, 12 January 1921, F.O. 371/6582, F 120/2/10, PRO. A week later Lampson expressed the same sentiment, declaring "that fatal Vickers contract is our undoing." See the minutes under Craigie to Curzon, 19 January 1921, F.O. 371/ 6582, F 251/2/10, PRO.

34. Wellesley minute under Davis to Curzon, 10 January 1921, F.O. 371/6582, F 120/2/10, PRO.

35. Jordan minuted under a letter from Handley Page asking that the Foreign Office register the 1920 contract to sell 105 planes to China: "It is, in my opinion, a suicidal policy to give any encouragement to transactions of this kind and we should, I think, come to an understanding with the other Powers at Peking to treat aeroplanes as war material and refuse to supply them to China under present conditions. The history of the Handley Page machines already supplied to China shows that all such aeroplanes will be used to promote internal trouble and will expose us to the charge of failing to observe the arrangement regarding war material." See the minutes under Handley Page to the Foreign Office, 3 January 1921, F.O. 371/6582, F 46/2/10, PRO. Ultimately Washington accepted the British position, at least in part because no American firm was inclined to conclude a major aircraft contract with China. See Pugach, "Aircraft," pp. 369-70.

36. Geddes to Curzon, 26 February 1921, F 701/2/10, DBFP, 1st ser., vol. 14, p. 257.

37. Hughes to Bell, 19 March 1921, 893.113/122a, FRUS 1921, pp. 552-53.

38. See the minute beneath Wright to Curzon, 22 March 1921, F.O. 371/6583, F 1106/2/10, PRO.

39. Hughes to Lodge, 14 March 1921, 693.119/444a, FRUS 1921, pp. 551-52.

40. See for example Hughes to Bell, 19 March 1921, 893.113/122a, FRUS 1921, pp. 552-53.

41. Dearing to H. A. Astlett & Co., 27 May 1921, 893.113/147, DSNA.

42. See K.V.V. Casey to Hughes, 17 June and 19 July 1921, Hughes to Casey, 11 August 1921, 893.113/151, DSNA.

43. Hughes to Geddes, 24 March 1921, 893.113/118, FRUS 1921, p. 554. Ruddock to Hughes, 28 June 1921, 893.113/169, DSNA. Not only arsenal equipment, but also aircraft were sent to Canton via Manila. In an attempt to end this traffic, the State Department requested that the acting governor general of the Philippines do nothing to encourage shipments of munitions of war to China. See F. M. Dearing to the Secretary of War, 12 September 1921, 893.113/175, FRUS 1921, pp. 560-61.

44. Geddes to Hughes, 14 March 1921, 893.113/118, FRUS 121, pp. 550-51.

45. Hughes to Geddes, 18 April 1921, 893.113/132, FRUS 1921, pp. 555-56.

46. See Jenkin's reports in Schurman to Hughes, 20 October 1921, 893.113/199, DSNA.

47. Schurman to Hughes, 9 December 1921, 893.113/202, FRUS 1921, p. 562. The British took particular interest in this affair. As Curzon explained to Alston, the "Japanese Government have accordingly decided to instruct their Ambassador at Rome to make representations against this violation of [the] agreement, and urge that His Majesty's Ambassador should associate himself with [the] Japanese protest. If [the] facts are as stated, co-operation of His Majesty's Ambassador at Rome seems desirable not only to maintain [the] embargo on [the] supply of arms to China, but also to encourage [the] Japanese, who themselves showed signs of defection from [the] policy last February." Curzon to Alston, 9 December 1921, F.O. 405/233, F 4527/2/10, PRO.

48. Hughes to Child, 23 December 1921, 893.113/207, FRUS 1921, pp. 563-64.

49. Child to Hughes, 30 January 1922, 893.113/229, FRUS 1921, pp. 725-26.

50. Conference on the Limitation of Armaments, Washington, November 12, 1921--February 6, 1922, (Washington, D.C.: 1922), p. 1474.

51. Lampson to Curzon, 9 February 1922, F. O. 371/8000, F 847/110/110, PRO.

52. For the complete text of the joint resolution and Harding's subsequent proclamation, see FRUS 1922, pp. 726-27.

53. Fletcher to Child, 4 March 1922, 893.113/299, FRUS 1922, pp. 727-28.

54. Child to Hughes, 13 April 1922, 893.119/246, FRUS 1922, p. 728. At the request of the State Department, the Italians stated on 18 April that "no more deliveries will be made under contracts before or after [the] joint declaration [of 5 May 1919]." Child to Hughes, 18 April 1922, 893.113/249, FRUS 1922.

55. Child to Hughes, 24 July 1922, 893.113/318, and 22 September 1922, 893.113/352, FRUS 1922, pp. 737, 742.

8

Unsuccessful Attempts to Strengthen the Embargo

Even as the Italians moved toward dropping their reservation to the embargo in the spring of 1922, another clash in the Chinese civil war tested the agreement's integrity. Since the Anfu-Chihli war in July 1920, Chang Tso-lin and his Fengtien clique had maintained an uneasy equilibrium with the Chihli party in ruling northern and central China. But by the fall of 1921 Chang felt strong enough to challenge his former allies and began to conclude alliances with disparate elements, including Tuan Ch'i-jui and Sun Yat-sen, in order to defeat the Chihli party and its rising military star Wu P'ei-fu.[1]

How would the powers react to this evidence that the Chinese were as far as ever from a peaceful reunification of their country? Both the United States and Great Britain continued to maintain as impartial an attitude as possible toward the contending factions. For instance, when Reuters printed an article in April 1922 to the effect that the British Legation supported Wu in the impending conflict, Minister Alston immediately confronted the Japanese chargé d'affaires after learning that the source of the story was the Japanese Legation. Alston's work ultimately resulted in Reuter's publication of "an adequate dementi." At the same time, the conduct of the U.S. Legation satisfied Secretary of State Hughes, who complimented Ambassador Jacob Gould Schurman: "Your adherence to strict impartiality as between the two leaders accords fully with the Department's view that foreign nations should stand so far as possible aloof from the internal dissensions in China."[2]

While the attitude of the principal Western powers was no surprise, Washington and London closely scrutinized the Japanese response to the crisis. To all appearances, Japan cooperated with the West and maintained a neutral attitude. Tokyo, consistent with the Hara cabinet's decision in May 1921, did not support Chang's aspirations outside of Manchuria. Foreign Minister Uchida did not waver from this policy in the face of the impending Fengtien-Chihli war; he instructed Consul General Akatsuka Shosuke at Mukden to see that army officers did not disobey the government by assisting Chang.[3] Uchida also repeatedly pledged to the powers that Japan would maintain strict neutrality in the dispute.[4]

Unfortunately for the civilian government in Tokyo, Japanese military officers in general, and those serving in China in particular, believed that Chang should receive aid from Japan. The military apparently acted on these beliefs; in May 1922 Schurman informed Hughes that well-informed observers suspected that the Japanese were helping Chang.[5] Indeed, Chang needed all the assistance the Japanese offered, because Wu's troops routed the Fengtien army on 4 May 1922. In order to save the situation Chang personally rallied his troops at Luan-chou. With extensive assistance from his Japanese adviser Honjo Shigeru, who organized the defense of the town and who had the operational command in battle, Wu's advance was blunted. Although Chang had suffered a demoralizing setback, Wu did not win a decisive victory; to achieve this would have required pressing the attack and then pursuing Chang into Manchuria, which risked a clash with the Japanese, who were not likely to permit any military operations that could disrupt their interests in the northeast.[6]

The fact that Wu and Chang both had adequate weaponry for battle, when combined with recent evidence of Danish and German shipments of war material to China, emphasized the need to tighten the arms embargo.[7] Curzon, who believed that conditions in China made the embargo "more than ever desirable," informed Secretary of State Hughes that the British wanted "to place the embargo policy on a more satisfactory footing." Towards this end, London proposed to extend the scope of the agreement to include "materials and tools destined directly or indirectly for the manufacture of arms and munitions of war, arsenal equipment, and personnel to supervise or assist in the use or manufacture of such arms and munitions."[8] As a further indication of London's sincerity, the British also agreed with a previous American proposal to refrain from assisting Chinese naval development.[9]

Hughes appreciated the British position and was "deeply gratified" by London's acceptance of the embargo on naval assistance. The United States was, however, reluctant to strengthen the arms embargo beyond the formula "arms or munitions of war, whether complete or in parts" proposed at the

Washington Conference. Hughes explained that the U.S. government, while not opposed to the spirit of the British proposal, could by law only prohibit the exportation to China of "arms and munitions of war."[10]

In spite of Hughes' warning, the Foreign Office was convinced that some way had to be found to strengthen the embargo. On 20 July 1922, citing the fact that various powers had ascribed "different interpretations" to the agreement, London proposed that the Diplomatic Corps at Peking review the situation "in order that the embargo may be not only reaffirmed but if thought desirable extended and more precisely defined."[11] Hughes recognized the need to make the embargo more effective and did not discourage the British initiative. However, he warned both the Foreign Office and Minister Schurman that the U.S. government faced a difficult, and perhaps impossible, task of obtaining any further legislation from Congress to enforce an expanded embargo.[12]

With this reservation in mind, Schurman discussed the embargo with his colleagues on 3 October 1922. While the ministers unanimously approved the Washington Conference formula embargoing "arms or munitions of war whether complete or in parts," they could not agree on language to strengthen the prohibition any further. However the diplomats did agree to submit to their governments for further consideration an interpolation which declared that the agreement was "understood to include aircraft *other than commercial aircraft* [emphasis added] and machinery and materials destined exclusively for the manufacture of arms or the equipment of arsenals."[13]

The work of the Diplomatic Corps did not particularly satisfy either London or Washington because the proposed interpolation expressly permitted the sale of commercial aircraft. Hughes was especially surprised by this statement and asked Schurman what attitude the British and the Japanese had taken on the issue. Ominously, Schurman replied that the French minister had insisted on this exemption in spite of British and Japanese opposition.[14]

For his part, Schurman was discouraged not only with the diplomats' work, but with the state of affairs in China. The legation had constantly received reports of Chang's ability to buy arms from abroad, and apparently little could be done to prevent it. Thus Schurman soured on the embargo, explaining to Hughes that presently the only effect of the agreement was to prevent certain factions from getting weapons. Therefore he asked "should an embargo be continued which binds [the] Chinese Government and leaves rebels (such as Chang Tso-lin, who had declared independence from Peking in May 1922) free?"[15] Hughes answered Schurman with an affirmation of the embargo: "[The] Department has believed [the] embargo to be a policy calculated to benefit China as a whole if consistently applied over [a] considerable period and would not feel warranted in changing such [a] policy on account of the incidental strength of a faction whose leadership may not appear so commendable as the present government. To do so would possibly expose this government to a suspicion of partisanship."[16] Hughes and the State Department believed that an imperfect embargo was better than no embargo at all; therefore, while Washington recognized that some powers could abuse the provision allowing the shipment of commercial planes, the United States accepted the work of the Peking diplomats, including the interpolation, in the hope that further discussion would result in a complete embargo of aircraft.[17]

Like his American colleague, Minister Alston had presented London with a negative assessment of the embargo. Alston believed that the embargo was a farce because there was no lack of arms in China. He concluded that while the embargo may have saved the Chinese some money, the agreement had had little effect on stopping the country's civil war.

One's distance from China, however, apparently altered one's perspective of the embargo; within the Foreign Office, some officials mirrored Hughes' optimism about the agreement's usefulness. These British supporters of the embargo realized that at the very least it had prevented a much larger flow of arms into China; furthermore Italy's apparent acceptance of the agreement and the inclusion of military aircraft and arsenal equipment in the Diplomatic Corp's interpolation represented recent progress.[18] Although London was disappointed that the Peking ministers had not expanded the embargo, for the British, there was little to do other than to solicit pledges of support for the agreement. But many powers, reluctant to see lucrative arms contracts go to foreign nationals, would do so only if all other countries likewise agreed.

Although the embargo's flaws were apparent and the cooperation of small powers was usually difficult to obtain, no power had yet made a serious effort to terminate the agreement. If the embargo was not effective as a method of ending the Chinese civil war, neither was it perceived to be working against American or British interests. Washington and London therefore continued to request that other powers adhere to the agreement, police their own nationals, and condemn Italy for fresh violations.[19]

As the powers looked vainly for a way in which to establish unanimity concerning the embargo, Chang Tso-lin busily evaded it, girding for a rematch with Wu P'ei-fu. This alarmed the civilian government in Tokyo, which again sought to prevent Japanese advisers from aiding Chang. The cabinet recognized that the intervention of Japanese military officers in the spring 1922 Fengtien-Chihli war, violating the strict neutrality proclaimed by the ministry of foreign affairs, had seriously embarrassed Japan vis-à-vis the other powers: "In this situation, with the Imperial Government constantly being put into a disadvantageous position in its diplomatic relations and having always to be making explanations, the harm that Japan suffers is probably incalculable. The recent behavior of Chang Tso-lin's Japanese . . . military attachés in the Fengtien-Chihli war is certainly an apposite example."[20] Ultimately, however, civilian officials were unwilling, or unable, to rectify the problem of military insubordination; Tokyo merely reiterated that officers in China should act in accordance with their instructions. In spite of this attempted reaffirmation of civilian control, the Japanese military would again intervene in Chinese affairs during the second Fengtien-Chihli war in the fall of 1924. The military did, however, apparently observe their orders not to assist Chang in the eighteen months preceding the conflict, because the prospect of hostilities led him to make an urgent appeal to Tokyo for aid.[21]

The new Japanese minister of foreign affairs, Shidehara Kijuro, did not honor Chang's request. Shidehara, upon assuming his portfolio in June 1924, had announced that Japan would continue to pursue a policy of nonintervention in China's internal affairs. Not only did he publicly repeat these declarations in September, but as the likelihood of combat increased, he also issued similar private admonitions to Consul General Funatsu Tatsuichiro in Mukden and the governor of Kwantung province Kodama Hideo.[22] Unfortunately, as the British Foreign Office well understood, the military did not automatically obey the instructions of the Japanese government. One Foreign Office official, in commenting on one of Shidehara's statements denying any intervention in Chinese affairs, minuted:

This is what we would expect from the Japanese Foreign Office; but unfortunately it is just at these crises that the independent policy of the General Staff has to be reckoned with. Hitherto it has been the General Staff's policy to favor Chang Tso-lin; and they can hardly abandon him completely if he gets the worst of it in the coming fight. Through the Japanese officers in Chinese service throughout China, they will exert influence in favor of Chang Tso-lin.[23]

Actual Chihli-Fengtien hostilities commenced in mid-September 1924.

After a series of Fengtien victories, fighting bogged down with neither side able to gain a decisive advantage over the other. Finally, in an attempt to break the deadlock, on 11 October Wu personally took command of the Chihli forces at the front near the town of Shan-hai-kuan.

The continuing stalemate on the battlefield increased concerns that a Chihli victory could endanger Japan's position in Manchuria. In spite of demands from some cabinet members to intervene, Shidehara steadfastly refused to send Japanese troops to China in order to relieve Chang's armies. At a cabinet meeting on 23 October, at the height of the Chang-Wu conflict, he argued that Japan's policy of nonintervention was a matter of public record and warned that "whether or not international confidence is kept is a grave matter affecting the fate of the nation." Shidehara's stance against intervention was not, however, tantamount to a renunciation of Japan's special interests in Manchuria. He tried to convince his colleagues that the situation in China was neither a military nor a political threat to Japan:

Even if Wu P'ei-fu were to follow up his victories by invading the Three Eastern Provinces, he must cross the South Manchuria Railroad to move his forces into Fengtien [province]. Since Japan has by treaty the right to station troops in the railway area, he can only cross it after doing battle with and defeating our railway guards. And in the case of the Chihli army approaching Fengtien after a long march, I doubt if they would have the strength left to meet our crack forces in the fire of battle. And even if Wu P'ei-fu were to rule Manchuria, it is by no means impossible that we could bring him to respect our established rights, in the same way as Chang Tso-lin.[24]

Thus Shidehara would not sanction active intervention on Chang's behalf.[25]

Japan nevertheless played a decisive role in the second Fengtien-Chihli war, most importantly in the form of a large bribe to one of Wu's subordinates. After learning that General Feng Yü-hsiang's allegiance could be purchased, the South Manchuria Railway Company loaned between 1 to 2.5 million yen to Chang, who passed the money to Feng through Japanese intermediaries. On 23 October 1924 Feng executed his coup d'etat, and moved his troops to threaten the Chihli rear. Wu had no choice but to retreat, extricating what units he could from the debacle.[26]

In the ensuing months Chang and Feng consolidated their control in the North; Feng became defense commissioner of the northwest; Chang accepted a similar post in the northeast, and Tuan Ch'i-jui became provisional chief executive. The extension of Chang's influence from Manchuria to the Yangtze in 1925 was not greeted with unanimous approval in Japan. Except to a minority of Japanese policy makers, Chang's primary role was to preserve stability in Manchuria, and not attempt to rule the whole country.

Prescient Japanese had recognized that a decisive victory by Chang in the fall of 1924 could work to Tokyo's disadvantage. Sir Charles Eliot had informed the Foreign Office in October 1924 that it was believed at the ministry of foreign affairs that "if Chang were to capture Peking and set up a new Government there he would probably escape from Japanese tutelage. There is no reason to believe that he has any real love, or admiration for this country, or that, if he were a safe distance from Japan, he would favor Japanese rather than other foreign interests."[27] Furthermore such an increase in Chang's power was bound to increase the fears and jealousies of Chinese rivals, which could result in combinations threatening to Japanese interests in China.

The second Fengtien-Chihli war not only increased Chang Tso-lin's power in China, but the scope of hostilities underscored again the inadequacies of the arms embargo as a tool to dampen the civil war. On 29 October 1924 the Foreign Office decided to "stir up" the U.S. government, believing that the time was ripe for all the powers to adopt formally the Washington Conference formula embargoing "arms or munitions of war whether complete or in parts" and the interpolation of the Peking Diplomatic Corps.[28] In this case French activity had also spurred the British government; just prior to the Fengtien-Chihli rematch the French mail steamer *Chantilly* had allegedly delivered military aircraft and machine guns to Chang's forces. In the face of this "grave breach of the whole spirit of the embargo agreement" Ambassador Sir Esme Howard asked Hughes to instruct the U.S. representative at Paris to associate with his British colleague "in addressing strong representations" to the French government.[29]

After investigation in Paris, however, the U.S. Chargé d'Affaires Sheldon Whitehouse concluded the French had violated only the spirit, not the letter, of the arms agreement by delivering to Chang commercial aircraft capable of conversion to military use. Whitehouse suggested to the British minister that since it would take too long to adopt a more strict definition of "commercial" aircraft, perhaps the interested powers could agree instead to embargo all airplane shipments to China until political conditions there improved. Believing that Whitehouse had a good idea, Foreign Secretary Austen Chamberlain proposed that the powers negotiate a gentleman's agreement to prohibit absolutely the export of all aircraft to China.[30]

Within the course of a week, however, Washington dashed London's hopes both for a stronger embargo and a gentleman's agreement concerning aircraft. On 20 December 1924 Hughes informed Ambassador Howard that Washington could only support a proposal restraining the powers from exporting aircraft to China "in so far as their respective laws and regulations will permit."[31] Hughes recognized that Washington's qualified acceptance fell short of the absolute prohibition London intended and explained that "this Government would, under existing legislation, find it difficult to obligate itself in the matter without reservation concerning the legal limitations of its competence with regard to the export of aircraft."[32] From the Foreign Office's perspective, Hughes had rendered the proposal of a gentleman's agreement worthless, since the French still would not be bound to prohibit the export of commercial aircraft that could be adapted to military purposes.[33]

Four days later Hughes again disappointed the Foreign Office. At that time he questioned whether there would now be any practical benefit to substituting the revised Washington formula for the agreement of May 1919, since to do so would mean losing the adherence of the Netherlands and Brazil; both had signed the original embargo, but did not show any willingness to adopt the more recent agreement. Even more importantly, Hughes noted that since neither London nor Washington could enforce that portion of the interpolation pertaining to arsenal equipment, both governments would have to qualify their acceptance of the 1922 formula. Hughes regretted that attempts to secure unanimity concerning the embargo had not succeeded, but he nevertheless concluded with an optimistic assessment of the agreement:

From a survey of the actual working of the Agreement of May, 1919, it is the view of this Government that the precise formula in use has been of less importance than the intent and spirit of the various governments concerned in carrying out the Agreement entered into at that time. In spite of the infractions of the embargo which have occurred from time to time, this Government is of the opinion that the embargo has attained a measurable success, and it desires in every way to strengthen its effectiveness.[34]

The American position gravely disappointed the British, since Hughes' attitude indicated that London's attempt to tighten the arms embargo had definitely failed.

Washington's disinclination to take any action angered some officials within the Foreign Office and led them to question whether there was any point in continuing efforts to solicit support for the agreement. Others launched even more scathing attacks:

The U.S. Government are, as usual, a broken reed when it comes to the point; and they merely add insult to injury by saying that the present agreement "has proved reasonably effective," in the face of all our evidence to the contrary. . . . I submit that the time has come when we must seriously consider what object is served by the continuance of the embargo, which can be set against its obvious disadvantages. I cannot see how the removal of the embargo would make matters in China any worse than they are already.[35]

In spite of such opinions, why would the British decide not to terminate the embargo?

One of the most convincing arguments in favor of maintaining the agreement came from the War Office early in 1925. In a report of 23 January, the Army Council expressed concern at the amount of weaponry reaching China, which represented "a serious menace" to foreigners and could lead to the need for additional military commitments in that country. Most alarming was evidence that the increase in armaments had changed the very nature of warfare in China. The council remarked that in the past "operations were carried out with considerable regard for the safety of the combatants and the losses incurred were slight." However, machine guns had been used with effect in fighting near Shanghai the previous October, which indicated that Chinese troops not only had learned how to use modern weaponry, but were prepared to suffer losses in combat. Thus a Chinese attack against foreign settlements could require military aid "on a scale not hitherto reckoned with."[36]

The Foreign Office accepted the War Office's report as both pertinent and sound. There was of course some resentment towards the French and nationals of minor powers who expected, and received, British military protection in spite of the fact that their arms sales threatened the security of all foreigners in China. Nevertheless the British resolved to do everything possible to maintain and improve the embargo.[37]

London communicated its decision to press on with the embargo to the new Secretary of State Frank B. Kellogg in March 1925. In so doing the British took the high moral ground, noting that London's "stringent administrative measures" had penalized British merchants and benefitted their Continental competitors. Chamberlain also pointed out that the arms traffic threatened the position of all foreigners in China:

In the opinion of His Majesty's Government the Powers, so long as they are unable or unwilling effectively to prevent their nationals from making money out of a traffic that merely increases the miseries of the Chinese people, are exposed to some measure of moral reproach and are in a position less strong than they would be other wise to deal with the calumnies of the agitators who exasperate anti-foreign feeling by representing the sufferings of China as due to the "imperialism" and greed of foreigners.

London asked Washington for suggestions "to find an exit from the present impasse" regarding the flow of arms into China, and hinted that one solution might be the scheduling of the country as a "prohibited area" at the forthcoming conference on arms traffic at Geneva in May 1925.[38]

Unfortunately for London, the new secretary of state was no more receptive to British overtures than his predecessor. Kellogg explained that the purpose of the Geneva conference was to look into the international arms trade rather than proposals to remedy the conditions prevailing in China. Furthermore, he added that Washington was not inclined to support the designation of China as a "prohibited area" since "such a proposal would serve merely as an irritant without tending toward a more effective supervision of the trade in arms with that country."[39] Thus the United States remained unwilling to work for new ways to end the flow of arms into China. Washington would not take action in support of the agreement beyond policing its own nationals and pointing out to Paris that the French should sell no aircraft to China because commercial aviation did not exist there.

Soon the British were to have more pressing concerns than the passive American attitude towards the arms embargo. On 30 May 1925 British police fired into a mob threatening a police station in the International Concession at Shanghai, killing several Chinese. A wave of anti-British and anti-foreign sentiment swept over most of China and benefitted the anti-imperialist bolsheviks, who posed the next serious threat to the China arms embargo.

NOTES

1. McCormack, pp. 62-64.

2. Hughes to Schurman, 17 May 1922, 893.00/4362, FRUS 1922, p. 706. Alston to Curzon, 24 April 1922, F.O. 371/7997, F 1514/84/10, PRO.

3. On 19 January 1922 Uchida sent the following explanation to Akatsuka: "1. In Chinese political affairs at present Chang's position is, as a leading warlord, not popular either among the people or with foreign countries, and it seems, in the light of the Washington Conference, that a position such as his will become more and more difficult and it is extremely questionable whether he will be able to maintain it or not. 2. Support of Chang would

mean that Japan would have to face great dangers. It is hard to believe that the fact of arms supply could remain undiscovered. . . . Further, it is possible that Chang might, in self-defense, advertise that he had Japanese support. And whatever else happened, if news of that got out, Japan would attract the criticisms and opposition not just of Chang's political enemies but of the Chinese people and world opinion, compromising our foreign and diplomatic relations. Also English and American support for Wu P'ei-fu in retaliation for Japanese support for Chang would lead to an Anglo-Japanese confrontation. Is it necessary to support Chang to the point of risking such dangers? . . . 4. Apart even from the above points, supply of arms to Chang would be an infringement of the agreement between the powers relating to embargo on the supply of arms to China, and would be contrary to the politics of neutrality, impartiality and nonintervention hitherto proclaimed and carefully adhered to by the Japanese government. Therefore, I do not at present see any necessity for Japan to depart from the policies followed till now." Quoted in McCormack, pp. 65-66.

4. For example see Eliot to Curzon, 19 May 1922, F.O. 371/8036, F 1797/1797/10, PRO. B.C. Newton minuted that "the Japanese Government are evidently very anxious that the suspicions of Japanese intentions in China, which were so largely removed by her attitude at the Washington Conference, should not be revived by the recent happenings in China, and the rumors to which they have given rise."

5. Schurman to Hughes, 13 May 1922, 893.00/4362, FRUS 1922, pp. 702-4. Three weeks later Alston betrayed a healthy skepticism of the Japanese declarations of neutrality: "[The] Japanese have hitherto done nothing overtly unneutral but have been almost suspiciously profuse in protestations of impartiality." Alston to Curzon, 4 June 1922, F.O. 371/8037, F 1928/1797/10, PRO.

6. McCormack, pp. 70-72. In the aftermath of his defeat, Chang declared Manchuria independent from the rest of China. Clive reported in August that the Japanese were again suspected of complicity: "The feeling is prevalent amongst foreign residents in Manchuria that the Japanese are doing all in their power below the surface to assist Chang Tso-lin in establishing an independent state, which must necessarily fall to all intents and purposes under Japanese protection." Clive to Curzon, 10 August 1922, F.O. 371/7998, F 3071/84/10, PRO.

7. For Danish and German activities, see Schurman to Hughes, 27 November 1921, 893.113/196, and 17 December 1921, 893.113/206,

DSNA; see also Alston to Curzon, 20 October 1921, F.O. 371/6646, F 4407/838/10, and 27 December 1921, F.O. 405/233, F 4812/838/10, PRO.

8. Harvey to Hughes, 24 May 1922, 893.34/174, FRUS 1922, p. 751. See also Curzon to Alston, 16 May 1922, F.O. 405/236, F 923/110/10, PRO.

9. Harvey to Hughes, 24 May 1922, 893.34/174, FRUS 1922, p. 751. See Department of State to the Japanese Embassy, 4 May 1922, 893.34/170a, FRUS 1922, pp. 747-48.

10. Hughes to Harvey, 2 June 1922, 893.113/278, FRUS 1922, pp. 729-30.

11. Harvey to Hughes, 20 July 1922, 893.113/313, FRUS 1922, pp. 736-37.

12. Hughes to Schurman, 24 July 1922, 893.113/249, FRUS 1922, pp. 737-38, Department of State to the British Embassy, 22 September 1922, 893.113/348, FRUS 1922, pp. 741-42.

13. Schurman to Hughes, 4 October 1922, 893.113/361, FRUS 1922, pp. 742-43.

14. Hughes to Schurman, 12 October 1922, 893.113/363; Schurman to Hughes, 24 October 1922, 893.113/374, FRUS 1922, pp. 743-44.

15. See Schurman to Hughes, 30 September 1922, 893.113/357 and 4 October 1922, 893.113/362, DSNA.

16. Hughes to Schurman, 12 October 1922, 893.113/362, DSNA. Nine months later Hughes reaffirmed his beliefs, noting that "the Department feels that, although the embargo of May 5, 1919, may not have been entirely effective, and although a majority of the Powers may not have the legal authority to effect a complete enforcement of its terms, it has nevertheless proved distinctly beneficial and is justified by its results." Hughes to Schurman, 16 July 1923, 893.113/511a, FRUS 1923, pp. 610-11.

17. Memorandum of the Division of Far Eastern Affairs, 2 November 1922, 893.113/386, DSNA. Hughes to Schurman, 6 November 1922, 893.113/380, FRUS 1922, pp. 744-45.

18. For Alston's opinions, see Alston to Curzon, 4 and 7 October 1922, F.O. 405/237, F 3433/110/10, PRO. For more optimistic assessments, see the minutes of C. F. Ashton-Warner under Alston to Curzon, 4 October 1922, F.O. 371/8002, F 3433/110/10, and F. Ashton-Gwatkin's minutes under Alston to Balfour, 5 October 1922, F.O. 371/8001, F 3133/110/10, PRO. By the end of the year, however, both Ashton-Warner and Ashton-Gwatkin were discouraged and used the word "farce" in association with the embargo. See minutes under Clive to Curzon, 27 December 1922, F.O. 371/9196, F 389/48/10, PRO.

19. For the efforts to secure the support of the smaller powers such as

Norway, Denmark, Sweden, Brazil, Spain, and Peru, see FRUS 1923, pp. 609-16. By the fall of 1922 the Italians again adopted an uncooperative attitude towards the embargo. In September Alston reported a statement by the Italian Chargé d'Affaires Vittorio Cerruti, who apparently remarked "why not let the Chinese have all the arms they want and fight it out. Perhaps high explosive shells will frighten them and they will think better of it." Alston to Curzon, 3 September 1922, F.O. 371/8001, F 3188/110/10. Such a cynical attitude towards the embargo, as well as a manner suggesting that Italy was not to be trifled with, led the legation to report that Cerruti did "not inspire much confidence" among his colleagues. Clive to Curzon, 8 February 1923, F.O. 405/240, F 862/862/10. By the summer of 1923 the Italians again sold arms to the Chinese, and Ashton-Gwatkin minuted under Rome's official denial that "the Italian reply is terse and mendacious." Victor Wellesley added, "Yes, it has not even the merit of being mellifluous." Graham to Curzon, 13 September 1923, F.O. 371/9198, F 2771/48/10. See also Macleay to Curzon, 12 June 1923, F.O. 371/9198, F 2168/48/10, PRO.

20. Cabinet decision of 22 July 1922, quoted in McCormack, p. 123.

21. Ibid., p. 127.

22. Ibid., pp. 139-41.

23. F. Ashton-Gwatkin minute under Eliot to MacDonald, 28 September 1924, F.O. 371/ 10244, F 3236/19/10, PRO.

24. Quoted in McCormack, p. 142.

25. The Foreign Office recognized that Japanese declarations that they did not in fact protect Chang from harm in Manchuria were not valid. Under one of them a Foreign Office official minuted: "This statement about not guaranteeing Chang Tso-lin's territory is rather disingenuous, considering that it is well-known that, after the last civil war, in which Chang Tso-lin was defeated by Wu P'ei-fu, the Japanese gave the latter to understand that they would not tolerate hostilities which might affect Japanese interests in Manchuria--which meant, in practice, that Wu could not follow up his success by marching on Mukden." Collier minute under Eliot to Chamberlain, 5 September 1924, F.O. 371/10244, F 3035/19/10, PRO.

26. McCormack, pp. 132-33, 143. On page 134 McCormack wrote: "It is clear . . . that the Japanese military at all levels did what could be done to aid Chang Tso-lin and to see Wu defeated, paying scant regard to the official Japanese line on the war."

27. Eliot to MacDonald, 3 October 1924, F.O. 410/77, F 3582/19/10, PRO.

28. MacDonald to Howard, 29 October 1924, F.O. 371/10241, F 3754/15/10, PRO. See also Howard to Hughes, 29 October 1924, 893.113/757, FRUS 1924, pp. 531-33. Just two months before, Schurman had commented that, "It is regrettable that the attempts to secure international agreement as to an arms embargo and the withholding of naval assistance to China to be concurred in by all the nations represented in Peking, seem to have proved abortive or, at best, most difficult to carry through to a successful conclusion." Schurman to Hughes, 26 July 1924, 893.113/729, DSNA.

29. Howard to Hughes, 24 October 1924, 893.113/755, FRUS 1924, pp. 530-31.

30. Whitehouse also informed Washington that the British minister had shown him the text of London's note "which was rather stiff in tone and has obviously annoyed the French." Whitehouse to Hughes, 14 November 1924, 893.113/769, DSNA (for a paraphrase, see FRUS 1924, pp. 533-34). Howard to Hughes, 20 November 1924, 893.113/772, FRUS 1924, p. 536.

31. Hughes to Howard, 20 December 1924, 893.113/784, FRUS 1924, pp. 540.

32. Ibid., p. 541.

33. See the Collier and Mill minutes under Howard to Chamberlain, 23 December 1924, F.O. 371/10242, F 4378/15/10, PRO.

34. Hughes to Howard, 24 December 1924, 893.113/787, FRUS 1924, pp. 543.

35. Collier minute under Howard to Chamberlain, 27 December 1924, F.O. 371/10242, F 4382/15/10, PRO. See also the minutes under Howard to Chamberlain, 23 December 1924, F.O. 371/10242, F 4378/15/10, as well as those under Howard to Chamberlain, 26 December 1924, F.O. 371/10915, F 43/1/10, PRO.

36. War Office to the Foreign Office, 23 January 1925, F.O. 405/247, F 321/1/10, PRO.

37. See the minutes under War Office to the Foreign Office, 23 January 1925, F.O. 405/247, F 321/1/10, PRO. Before making this decision, Chamberlain had solicited the opinion of Minister Ronald Macleay, declaring that it was "desirable to find [a] substitute for [the] arms embargo policy, which is almost [a] complete failure." Macleay sharply disagreed with Chamberlain: "In spite of its failure to prevent all importation of arms, [the] embargo policy has undoubtedly prevented enormous dumping of war material in China by British, American, Japanese and French armament

firms, and I do not think that it can be considered [an] almost complete failure." See Chamberlain to Macleay, 6 February 1925, F.O. 371/10915, F 481/1/10, and Macleay to Chamberlain, 14 February 1925, F.O. 405/247, F 572/1/10, PRO.

38. See Howard to Kellogg, 12 March 1925, 893.113/818 and Howard to Kellogg 16 March 1925, 893.113/820, FRUS 1925, pp. 641-644. Britain's moral reasons for continuing the embargo had both supporters and opponents within the Foreign Office. On 23 February G. Moss minuted "our arms embargo policy will satisfy our own conscience, the international conscience and the League of Nations--we shall get no gratitude elsewhere, least of all from China." L. Collier responded: "I have not noticed any very active international conscience about the arms traffic in China, and I think . . . it is not advisable to give it more than the absolute minimum of satisfaction." See the minutes under Macleay to Chamberlain, 23 February 1925, F.O. 371/10918, F 1427/2/10, PRO.

39. Kellogg to Chamberlain, 15 April 1925, 500 A.14/167a, FRUS 1925, p. 646.

9

The Soviet Challenge and the Termination of the China Arms Embargo

The Soviet Union posed the most serious threat to the China arms embargo during the agreement's final four years. At this time the embargoing powers were forced to confront the possibility that the embargo worked to the advantage of Moscow, which flouted the agreement by supporting pro-bolshevik factions in China. The question debated was whether or not lifting the embargo would serve or harm the interests of the embargoing powers and the prospects of the anti-bolshevik Chinese factions.

Even though British investment in China was the greatest of all the powers, the Foreign Office had not initially viewed the possibility of the spread of bolshevism into China with much concern. As late as January 1925, the head of the Foreign Office Far Eastern Department, Sir Victor Wellesley, could write, "I do not think that Bolshevism will ever [get?] a real hold over so conservative people as the Chinese." Wellesley conceded, however, that the Soviet Embassy might achieve a short-lived political domination in the country that could do "an incalculable amount" of damage while it lasted.[1] Nevertheless, since the Soviets were not yet perceived to pose a serious threat, officials such as Minister Ronald Macleay in Peking could dismiss Chang Tso-lin's appeals for Western aid to battle bolshevism as mere camouflage to secure assistance to fight his Chinese opponents.[2]

By February 1925, however, British perceptions of the Chinese situation began to change in the face of mounting evidence of Soviet arms shipments to China. For his part, Wellesley, while still not believing the sincerity of Chang's anti-bolshevik rhetoric, now admitted that a situation could conceivably arise in which the powers would consider lifting the embargo in order to check the spread of Soviet influence.[3] At the lower levels of the

Foreign Office, however, the Soviet shipments provided opponents of the embargo with new ammunition to attack an agreement they believed at the very least made Chang pay more for his weapons and at the worst benefitted his political adversaries.[4]

London's attitude toward the embargo became a much more pressing issue when British prestige in China declined sharply in the spring of 1925. The Shanghai incident in May sparked a series of anti-British protests, which resulted in the deaths of over fifty more Chinese in June when British and French forces defended the Shameen concession in Canton from a hostile mob. Quickly, an anti-British boycott, which greatly disrupted British trade, spread through southern China and Hong Kong. Compounding the problem of what was believed to be Russian-inspired trouble in South China were accounts that the Soviets were supplying Feng Yü-hsiang in northwest China with war material on a large scale from Siberia. Would London's opinion of the embargo change in the face of such ominous circumstances?[5]

Predictably, the junior officials in the Foreign Office who had previously attacked the embargo continued to condemn the agreement for operating in favor of Feng and against Chang Tso-lin, who apparently was not receiving sufficient weaponry from the Japanese and French.[6] But Wellesley still refused to consider terminating the embargo: "I feel convinced that it would be most unwise for us to identify ourselves with any factions in China. For us to support Chang would be to weaken him and defeat our own ends."[7] Wellesley, no doubt recalling Tuan Ch'i-jui's loss of support within China after he was identified too closely with Japanese interests, feared that London would play into the hands of the bolsheviks if Great Britain raised the embargo in Chang's favor at the height of anti-British sentiment.[8] Furthermore those arguments in favor of ending the embargo in order to strengthen Chang Tso-lin as an anti-communist Chinese leader lost some of their force late in 1925, when Chang was nearly toppled from power in Manchuria.

The genesis of this Manchurian crisis was the Chang-Feng rivalry for control of northern China. Central to Feng's plan to unseat Chang was a rebellion from within the Fengtien army itself. In late November 1925 Feng signed an agreement with Kuo Sung-ling, the temporary commander of the best-trained and best-equipped units of the northeastern armies, which would have turned the Three Eastern Provinces over to Kuo upon a successful rebellion against Chang. In spite of the fact that Kuo's forces fought a winter campaign in summer dress, they won a startling series of victories, which led the British consul general at Mukden, F. E. Wilkenson, to report on 10 December that "the Japanese authorities are still convinced that it is all over with the marshall [Chang], and if we are to judge by the display made up to now by his generals and troops, the days of his authority must certainly be numbered."[9] Chang, too, had doubts about the future, for he made plans to seek protection in the Japanese-controlled South Manchuria Railway zone and apparently even contemplated suicide.[10]

As in the case of previous Manchurian crises, the attitude of the Japanese was decisive. After a meeting with the premier and war minister, Shidehara issued a warning on 8 December to both Chang and Kuo about the need to safeguard Japanese rights and interests during their conflict. Although Shidehara referred to Japan's policy of strict non-interference in Chinese affairs, he did declare that if an emergency should arise "recourse must be had to such steps as may be required by the circumstances."[11]

The Japanese military, however, fearing not only disruption in Manchuria, but the spread of Soviet influence as well, went even further than mere verbal warnings and assisted Chang during in the conflict. The first decisive Japanese intervention occurred on 13 December, as Kuo's forces approached the town of Ying-k'ou, which Chang's troops had recently abandoned. The Kwantung Army's commander, General Shirakawa Yoshinori, informed Kuo that his men could not cross the Liao River and occupy the town, thus effectively blocking one route of advance against Chang. Shirakawa took this step on his own initiative and did not remove the ban even when Shidehara instructed him to do so.[12]

Bolstered by such indications of continued Japanese support, Chang rallied his forces for the decisive battle only thirty miles from Mukden. With the assistance of the Japanese advisers in units of his army, as well as of a fifteen-inch heavy artillery unit manned by Japanese reservists under the command of a Japanese officer, Chang offered battle on 21 December. After two days of fighting, one of Chang's cavalry units managed to attack Kuo's forces from the rear and quickly routed the rebels. Kuo and his wife were captured and shot, and their bodies were displayed in Mukden on Christmas Day.[13]

Politically, Kuo's defeat also represented a blow to Feng Yü-hsiang, who had double-crossed both Chang Tso-lin and Wu P'ei-fu. Although Wu and Chang had previously fought two wars against each other, in mid-January 1926 they put aside their differences and formed an alliance against Feng. This coalition dominated northern China for the next two years, and Feng, who realized that the balance of forces had shifted against him, resigned all his offices and left the country for an extended trip in the Soviet Union.[14]

By early 1926, then, China was divided into two main contending factions: the Soviet-supported Kuomintang based mainly in the south, and the Chang-Wu alliance in the north. Given the threat to British interests that a Kuomintang victory presented, London pondered an appropriate response to the new situation in China during the first months of the year. As in the past, the central issue in the discussion was the continuation or termination of the embargo.

After extensive debate, British policy remained unchanged; London would retain the embargo and not take sides in the civil war. In January, however, many in the Foreign Office had hoped to improve not only Britain's image in China after the Shanghai and Shameen shootings but also the embargo's effectiveness by altering the nature of the embargo. As one Foreign Office functionary asked, "Instead of an agreement between the Powers to impose an embargo upon importing arms into China--thereby once again offending China's *amour propre* by publicly treating her as inferior--is it not possible for us to accept the Chinese law prohibiting [the] import of arms and making it binding on our nationals, and invite the other Powers to do the same?"[15] Unfortunately, as Minister Macleay pointed out, while the Chinese law prohibiting the import of arms was already binding on British subjects, the question of how far this prohibition bound other foreign nationals was a "matter of doubt." Furthermore Macleay added that the members of the powers' Extraterritoriality Commission were not inclined to discuss the matter, as London had suggested they might.[16]

In responding to London's initiative, Macleay revealed that he had misread the motives of the Foreign Office: he had concluded his telegram with the observation that "it seems that as [the] sole object of [the] modification of our embargo policy is to permit [the] supply of arms to anti-Bolsheviks we might reserve our attitude on this point for the time being."[17] As J. T. Pratt in the Foreign Office pointed out, Macleay had misunderstood London's position and had mistakenly believed that Great Britain contemplated reversing its time-honored policy of not backing any faction in China. Pratt listed several reasons why such a reversal would be "a profound mistake": (1) when word leaked out that Britain was aiding one leader (in this case Wu P'ei-fu), the extreme elements in China would unite against him; (2) pinning one's hopes on any of the leaders in establishing a strong central government in China was sheer folly; and (3) even if the embargo were raised once Wu gained Peking, what would London do if the communists subsequently overthrew him?[18] Thus Chamberlain informed Macleay on 13 March that London had contemplated altering the embargo not to supply anti-bolsheviks, but rather to enable British manufacturers to compete with other nationals in supplying war material to a future stable and friendly Chinese government.[19]

Secretary of State Kellogg essentially agreed with the Foreign Office, believing that the powers should maintain the embargo in spite of the advice to the contrary he received from China. In April 1926 Minister MacMurray had advised Washington that since the embargo did not measurably diminish warfare in China, it should be terminated. MacMurray's recommendations carried weight not only on the basis of the year he had spent as minister at Peking, but also because he had played a part in the establishment of the embargo in 1919. In presenting his case to Kellogg, MacMurray used arguments familiar in the Foreign Office:

Apart from this general ineffectiveness of the embargo is the particular question of [the] supply of arms by Russia to such forces as are willing to cooperate in Soviet policies in this country. This supply is on a large scale and, in the face of it, refusal to permit the sale of arms to the Government or to other factions becomes tantamount to intervention to their detriment. It is known that Chang Tso-lin and Wu P'ei-fu, for instance, strongly resent the restriction thus imposed upon them.[20]

Kellogg, however, while inclined to agree that the embargo had failed to restrict the supply of arms to China, did not believe that Washington should initiate a discussion of either revising or terminating the agreement, since Washington would be accused of having done so in order to favor one faction over another.[21]

Significantly, Kellogg reversed his opinion only four months later. On 30 July 1926 MacMurray had informed Washington that he believed that London now permitted British citizens to sell commercial aircraft to China. On 5 August Kellogg replied that the United States would take similar action if MacMurray could confirm his report. Kellogg, however, also instructed MacMurray that "you are authorized in your discretion to discuss [the] question of [the] possible cancellation [of the] China arms embargo."[22] Why this sudden reversal?

Surely, the British position on the sale of commercial aircraft to China could not have sparked such a dramatic shift in Kellogg's embargo policy. Much more crucial must have been events within China, for in the summer of

1926 Chiang Kai-shek's Kuomintang armies began their Northern Expedition to reunite the country. Chiang's forces rapidly advanced into the Yangtze Valley against Wu P'ei-fu, since Wu's main strength was concentrated against Feng's forces in northern China. Kellogg's apparent *volte-face* on the embargo when confronted with Chiang's success against anti-communist forces, however, came to nothing; MacMurray at first postponed taking action in order to discuss the matter with the British minister, who was absent from Peking, and then apparently chose not to pursue the matter at all.[23]

The Foreign Office was also forced to reconsider British policy as Chiang's Kuomintang forces advanced northward. One of the most vocal advocates of a reversal of British policy was Sir Charles Clementi, governor of Hong Kong, who was responsible for overseeing the extensive British interests on that island, which was so exposed to Kuomintang power. A month before the start of the Northern Expedition, in May 1926, Clementi, although believing it would be "foolishly quixotic" for Britain to refrain from assisting a friendly and stable Chinese government under attack from bolshevik-inspired extremists, had favored the policy of strict British neutrality since no central government existed in China.[24] Less than three months later, in early August, Clementi reversed his position. After Chiang's advances, Clementi believed that the arms embargo, if enforced by all countries except Russia could "only promote the rapid spread of Bolshevism." In a passage that illustrated Clementi's change of heart, he noted that while there still was no central government in China, the arms embargo "now only serves to make it less easy for anti-Bolsheviks than for Bolsheviks in China to obtain the arms and ammunition which they need, and, plainly, a policy which serves no better purpose than this ought without delay to be modified."[25] Ultimately, Clementi advocated such strong measures against the Kuomintang as to provoke one Foreign Office official to retort: "Is Sir C. Clementi H. M. Minister in China, or Governor of Hong Kong?"[26] In spite of Clementi's (and incidentally also Minister Macleay's) protests in the fall of 1926 that Chiang's successes necessitated an end to the embargo, the Foreign Office refused to budge.[27]

The British approach to the embargo, as well as to China as a whole, was tested again in early 1927. During the first days of January, a hostile mob influenced by the left wing of the Kuomintang attempted to force their way into the British concession at Hankow. Realizing that Nationalist troops could not keep order and that the Chinese could not be held back without firing upon them, the British abandoned the concession. Although the Nationalists allowed the British to resume control of Hankow several days later, London was apprehensive about what could happen at places such as Shanghai, where British interests were so great that no such withdrawal could be contemplated. Thus the Chiefs of Staff reported to the cabinet on 11 January that:

> The Nationalist Government, working to a considerable extent under Bolshevist influence, has obtained control of the greater part of China south of the Yangtze. . . . .
> We recognize that the magnitude of our interests at Shanghai and the reaction of a disaster there on our interests and prestige in other parts of China and of the whole East may be such as to compel us to an active defence. We admit the possibility also that by showing a bold front at Shanghai we may stop the rot. But we feel bound to point out that our attitude may lead to a war, the consequences and magnitude of which cannot be foreseen.[28]

The cabinet responded by sending twelve thousand troops to China in order to protect British lives and property.[29] The increased tensions in China, as well as Britain's expanded military commitments there, militated in favor of Great Britain's strict observation of the arms embargo. Chamberlain told the new minister to China, Sir Miles Lampson, that "if anything, our vigilance should be strengthened rather than relaxed in order to prevent in so far as we can the passage of any arms which might come to be used against our own troops by Chinese forces of either faction. Our precautions must also be directed quite impartially."[30]

In spite of London's actions, the feared incident occurred in Nanking on 24 March 1927, when Nationalist troops sacked the city, showing no regard for foreign lives or property. After a six-hour rampage in which three British subjects were killed, and the British, American, and Japanese consulates were pillaged, one British and two American ships shelled the city, quelling the riot.[31] In London the cabinet pondered ways to retaliate for the Nanking and Hankow attacks, but ultimately took no action. Chancellor of the Exchequer Winston Churchill wrote in disgust: "To fire off Naval cannon at obsolete Chinese forts, or worthless Chinese arsenals or ludicrous Chinese warships cannot lead to any lasting advantage. . . . Punishing China is like flogging a jellyfish."[32] Churchill's exasperation is perhaps understandable. By not retaliating and by maintaining the embargo, the British had avoided the temptation to take action and risk intervening in the civil war. In this instance, British patience was rewarded when Chiang Kai-shek, in the wake of the Nanking excesses, purged the communists from the Kuomintang and then expelled Russian advisers in the summer of 1927.

The British, while pleased with this turn of events in southern China, did not hurry to change their stance on the embargo in spite of Chiang's attack on the communists. In the middle of May Chamberlain wrote a memo for the cabinet in which he advised that Britain's neutrality policy continued to be correct since "nothing else has prevented us at one time or another from backing the wrong horse and it is still too soon to pick the winner."[33] The British position of impartiality became all the more necessary as the hopes for a Chang-Chiang compromise were dashed and each side girded for battle.

How would the United States and Japan react to the impending Chang-Chiang struggle? The British had long since decided that the United States would no longer play a leading role in Far Eastern affairs. On 25 December 1927 Lampson informed London that Minister MacMurray had painted a most discouraging picture upon his return to China from the United States: "A feeling of general disinterestedness in China amounting to almost boredom is noteworthy amongst the American public. . . . With this goes intense and quite blind and unreasonable suspicion of Great Britain and all British policy in the Far East. We are historically and actually the villains of the piece."[34] While this anti-British feeling was not found within the State Department, MacMurray had "entirely failed" to dissipate this sentiment wherever else he encountered it. Lampson's discouraging impression of American policy was reinforced in London. One Foreign Office official minuted under Lampson's report an account of an interview with a member of the U.S. Embassy staff, who gave the personal impression that the State Department had recalled MacMurray in order to impress upon him that "it was out of the question for them to carry on any active policy in China" because the American people were not interested in the country.[35]

In Japan, even before Chiang's purge of the Kuomintang, Shidehara had reacted to the Chinese situation under the assumption that neither the communists nor their Soviet advisers controlled the Nationalist movement. Instead he believed that the Kuomintang leaders around General Chiang Kai-shek could reasonably be expected to respect Japan's position in Manchuria, and indeed all of China. Therefore Shidehara argued that either increased numbers of foreign troops or increased pressure on the southern regime could only strengthen the hand of Chiang's left-wing opponents in the Kuomintang. Thus, although minor incidents between Chinese and Japanese might occur, he deemed non-interference to be the proper course in order to avoid major collisions with Chinese mobs. If the Kuomintang could not keep order and a large-scale incident loomed, Japanese residents would be moved either to the Japanese-policed concessions or, as a last resort, to naval vessels along the Yangtze or at Shanghai. Thus Shidehara sought to maintain as much of Japan's "special position" in China as possible by the process of negotiation and persuasion, rather than by force of arms.[36]

Such moderation and patience would have been difficult to maintain in the best of conditions, and Shidehara's policy fell easy prey to those advocating an active response to real or imagined insults to Japanese national honor. In light of the Nanking and Hankow incidents in the spring of 1927, calls for a more vigorous Japanese response had intensified. In April Army Minister Ugaki Kazushige told Premier Wakatsuki Reijiro that "passive measures" would no longer work in China and he proposed that Japan lead a coalition of powers against communism in China. If propaganda failed, he advocated a limited intervention by troops in key areas, as well as sending arms and funds to moderate Chinese factions.[37]

Ultimately, however, Shidehara had little opportunity to react to Ugaki's hard-line recommendations. In the wake of increasing friction over China policy and a financial panic that gripped the country, the Wakatsuki government resigned on 17 April. The new premier and foreign minister, Tanaka Giichi, had strongly opposed Shidehara's approach to Chinese affairs and believed that Japan should undertake what he termed a "positive" policy there. Although Shidehara had ordered the use of Japanese troops in response to local attacks on Japanese in Tsingtao in 1925 and Hankow in 1927, the fact that such attacks had occurred at all ultimately contributed to a loss of confidence in the government. The army, opposition political parties, and Japanese residents in China all clamored for a stronger foreign policy and the change from nonintervention to military intervention in Chinese affairs.[38]

Tanaka did decide to continue Shidehara's policy of seeking improved relations with China through Chiang and his faction of the Kuomintang. But having stated that Japanese and their property in China would be "protected on the spot," Tanaka pledged himself to a more interventionist policy than his predecessor. Tanaka made good on this promise on 24 May when the cabinet decided to send an expeditionary force to Tsingtao, not in the face of an impending crisis, but in case they should be needed to protect Japanese in Shantung province. These troops contributed little to the maintenance of peace, soured Sino-Japanese relations, were an embarrassment to Japan, and were finally withdrawn in August.[39]

The Shantung expedition also did, however, intrude on the political and military situation in China, because Japanese forces temporarily shielded Chang's troops from attack by the Nationalists. This satisfied Tanaka, since it meshed with his intention to find some way to reconcile the new China of Chiang Kai-shek with the old China of Chang Tso-lin. Unlike Shidehara, the new prime minister feared that Kuomintang influence could undermine Japanese interests if Chang was eliminated, so he continued to support the marshal as the guarantor of peace and Japanese prosperity in Manchuria.[40] Thus while Tanaka was quite willing to support a China unified under the non-communist Chiang Kai-shek, at the same time he also hoped to assist Chang Tso-lin preserve his local power base.[41]

Tanaka's goal of maintaining both Chiang and Chang had a direct impact on Japan's enthusiasm for the arms embargo. Undoubtedly reasoning that the flow of weapons into the country made a Chiang-Chang clash within Manchuria all the more likely, in January 1928 Tokyo took the initiative in proposing discussions at Peking to tighten the embargo. The Japanese now believed that Germany would join the agreement and that Tokyo could conclude a similar arrangement with Moscow. Chamberlain, while sympathetic to Japanese aspirations, believed that the embargo could never be watertight; nonetheless he supported the Japanese initiative.[42]

The State Department responded to the Japanese proposal without alacrity. Kellogg instructed Ambassador Charles MacVeagh to inform Tokyo that the United States welcomed an opportunity to review the whole question, but suggested that the Diplomatic Corps at Peking should first discuss the degree of success the agreement had obtained over the previous nine years. Kellogg's official reply to Tokyo was actually disingenuous, because Washington had all but decided that the embargo should be terminated. When Kellogg repeated the correspondence with MacVeagh to Chargé d'Affaires Ferdinand Mayer at Peking, he revealed his true opinion. He remarked that because of major changes in the international situation since 1919, the embargo had had only a slight effect in limiting the import of arms into China:

The Department would heartily support an international agreement designed to prevent the importation of arms into China if it could feel hopeful of the success of such a project. However, the lack of any effective cooperative authority in China and other obvious obstacles appear well nigh insuperable. The Department doubts whether it will be found possible so to strengthen and broaden the 1919 embargo agreement as to render advisable its continuance.[43]

Kellogg was not willing, however, to shoulder the responsibility for ending the embargo, and asked Mayer to avoid conveying the impression that Washington had arrived at any definitive conclusion.

Unfortunately for Kellogg, Mayer was unable to lead the Diplomatic Corps into a discussion aimed at ending the embargo. Instead, the diplomatic representatives drafted another identic telegram, asking their governments to take the necessary steps to make the embargo effective. Mayer joined with his colleagues in this effort in order to avoid the onus of obstructing alone such an international undertaking.[44]

Nevertheless Tanaka's attempt to invigorate the embargo and preserve the Chiang-Chang status quo in China failed. On the one hand, the powers were as far from unified action as ever; while Germany moved toward accepting the embargo, Czechoslovakia and the Soviet Union did not. On the other hand, events within China conspired against Tanaka's efforts to preserve Chang Tso-lin in Manchuria.[45]

Chiang resumed the Northern Expedition against Chang in April 1928, and before the end of the month had won a string of victories. By early May Chang ordered his armies to take up purely defensive positions, and at a conference in Peking on 31 May, he decided to withdraw his forces to the northeast. But Tanaka's desire to have Chang continue to rule Manchuria was shattered; on 4 June junior officers of the Kwantung army who were dissatisfied with Chang's attitude toward Japan assassinated the marshal by blowing up his Mukden-bound train.[46] This act of military insubordination ultimately worked against Tokyo's interests, for Chang's successor, his son Chang Hsüeh-liang, refused to become Japan's Manchurian agent. Chang Hsüeh-liang emphasized his independence from foreign tutelage when he reversed his father's policy and accepted Nationalist authority in Manchuria in spite of vigorous Japanese protests.

Given the uncertainty surrounding the way in which the Nationalists would view Japan's special interests in Manchuria, Tokyo was obviously reluctant to strengthen Chiang by terminating the arms embargo. For the balance of 1928, London supported Tokyo's efforts to sustain the agreement, believing its termination premature. However, by November the Diplomatic Corps at Peking realized that since the Nanking government had managed to establish its authority over much of the country, it would be difficult to refuse a request from Chiang to withdraw the embargo.[47]

By January 1929, after London recognized the Nanking government, British officials finally favored ending the embargo.[48] The next month

Lampson could report from Peking that except for the Japanese chargé d'affaires, there was "general and even emphatic opinion," that the time had come to end the embargo.[49]   Japanese hesitation managed to delay termination for two months, but the agreement's days were numbered when on 2 April Nanking requested that the embargo be raised. On 19 April the Diplomatic Corps voted unanimously to withdraw the embargo on 26 April 1929, allowing the agreement to pass unlamented into history after an existence of just under ten years.[50]

NOTES

1. Wellesley minute of 26 January 1925 under Macleay to Chamberlain, 29 November 1924, F.O. 371/10917, F 268/2/10, PRO. Chamberlain agreed with Wellesley's opinion, for the initials "AC" appear under the minute without additional comment.

2. For example, on 29 December 1924 Macleay wrote, "It is quite possible, and even probable, that Marshal Chang is making all the use he can of the Bolshevik menace to secure the support of the Powers for himself and his friends against their political opponents."   Macleay to Chamberlain, 29 December 1924, F.O. 371/10942, F 592/194/10, PRO.

3. Macleay to Chamberlain, 18 February 1925, F.O. 371/10915, F 1253/1/10, PRO. See also the 21 February minute of Wellesley under Macleay to Chamberlain, 29 December 1924, F.O. 371/10942, F 592/194/10, PRO. In a memo of 1 March 1925 on British policy in China, Wellesley wrote, "The Soviet policy of Russia is at present the most sinister influence in the Far East. It aims at freeing China from her treaty obligations and seeks to bring her within the orbit of the Soviet Union." See F.O. 405/247, F 952/190/10, PRO.

4. For example, see the minutes under Macleay to Chamberlain, 18 February 1925, F.O. 371/10915, F 1253/1/10, PRO.

5. William Roger Louis, *British Strategy in the Far East* (Oxford: 1971), pp. 126-29.   For British accounts of Soviet aid to Feng, see Paliaret to Chamberlain, 5 May 1925, F.O. 371/10919, F 2300/2/10, and the Collier minutes under a private letter to Waterlow, 4 June 1925, F.O. 371/10918, F 2082/2/10, PRO. For U.S. accounts, see Mayer to Kellogg, 24 April 1925, 893.113/839, and Stanton to Kellogg, 13 May 1925, 893.113/858, DSNA.

6. See for instance the minutes of B. C. Newton and L. Collier under

Paliaret to Chamberlain, 5 May 1925, F.O. 371/10919, F 2300/2/10, and the private letter to Waterlow of 4 June 1925, F.O. 371/10918, F 2082/2/10, PRO.

7. See the Wellesley minute under the F.O. minute by S. P. Waterlow, 25 June 1925, F.O. 371/10919, F 2575/2/10, PRO. Chamberlain minuted, "I agree" under Wellesley's remarks. A month later, Wellesley reiterated the same opinion: "The arms embargo policy must be considered strictly on its own merits and not with a view to helping any particular faction in China." See the Wellesley minute under Paliaret to Chamberlain, 14 July 1925, F.O. 371/10921, F 3140/2/10, PRO.

8. In a conversation with a representative of the French Embassy in London at the end of September, Waterlow expressed the same opinion: "If we lifted the embargo in favor of Chang Tso-lin, should we not become the objects of violent misrepresentations, both at home and in China, to the effect that we were supplying arms to an imperialist pro-foreign oppressor, thus harming our cause more than we should benefit it?" See the 30 September 1925 note of Waterlow, F.O. 405/248, F 4835/1/10, PRO.

9. See Wilkenson to Macleay contained in Macleay to Chamberlain, 4 January 1926, F.O. 405/250, F 637/10/10, PRO.

10. McCormack, pp. 162-65.

11. Ibid., p. 177.

12. Ibid., pp. 177-79.

13. Ibid., pp. 182-87.

14. Ibid., p. 205.

15. Pratt minute, quoted in Gwatkin minute of 25 February 1926, under Macleay to Chamberlain, 10 February 1926, F.O. 371/11672, F 544/184/10, PRO.

16. See Chamberlain to Macleay, 3 March 1926, F.O. 371/11672, F 544/184/10, and Macleay to Chamberlain, 10 March 1926, F.O. 371/11672, F 1025/184/10, PRO.

17. Macleay to Chamberlain, 10 March 1926, F.O. 371/11672, F 1025/184/10, PRO.

18. Pratt minute under Macleay to Chamberlain, 10 March 1926, F.O. 371/11672, F 1025/184/10, PRO.

19. Chamberlain to Macleay, 13 March 1926, F.O. 371/11672, F 1025/184/10, PRO. A month later, in order to end some of "the hardships from which British merchants" were suffering, Chamberlain told Macleay that "we are no longer attempting to regard . . . [commercial] aeroplanes as

munitions within the scope of the embargo, yet their importation is prohibited by the Chinese government except under special license, for which British firms should take care to apply." Chamberlain to Macleay, 13 April 1926, F.O. 405/251, F 1093/184/10, PRO.

20. MacMurray to Kellogg, 3 April 1926, 893.113/952, FRUS 1926, pp. 734.

21. Kellogg to MacMurray, 13 April 1926, 893.113/952, FRUS 1926, p. 735.

22. MacMurray to Kellogg, 30 July 1926, 893.113 Airplanes/1, and Kellogg to MacMurray, 5 August 1926, 893.113 Airplanes/2, FRUS 1926, pp. 735. See also note 9 above.

23. MacMurray to Kellogg, 3 September 1925, 893.113 Airplanes/3, FRUS 1926, p. 736. No reference to a meeting with the British minister was found in either American or British archives.

24. 9 March 1926, letter of Clementi to Amery, forwarded by the Colonial Office to the Foreign Office on 17 May 1926, F.O. 371/11673, F 2040/184/10, PRO.

25. 28 June 1926, letter of Clementi to Amery, forwarded by the Colonial Office to the Foreign Office on 7 August 1926, F.O. 405/252A, F 3179/10/10, PRO.

26. W. Stark Toller minute under a Clementi letter forwarded to the Foreign Office on 26 January 1927, F.O. 371/12400, F 802/2/10, PRO. Eventually, even the Colonial Office was ashamed of Clementi's tirades, for his letters were no longer forwarded to the Foreign Office, even when requested. Strang minuted on 29 August 1927 that "Mr. Johnson has made several attempts to persuade the Colonial Office to send us Sir C. Clementi's despatch but they have been reluctant to do so. I imagine that it is one of Sir C. Clementi's more amateurish excursions into foreign affairs and they are possibly a little ashamed of it." See the minutes under Tilley to Chamberlain, 30 March 1927, F.O. 371/12405, F 4278/2/10, PRO.

27. See the Gwatkin and Wellesley minutes under War Office to Foreign Office, 12 August 1926, F.O. 371/11673, F 3291/184/10, and Tyrrell to Macleay, 17 September 1926, F.O. 405/252A, unnumbered, PRO. It should be noted that Colonial Secretary Leopold S. Amery, vigorously defended Clementi. In a letter to Prime Minister Stanley Baldwin, Amery wrote, "In his official telegrams Clementi has expressed his disagreement [with Great Britain's China policy] pretty freely on more than one occasion, and both Austen and Lampson have not unnaturally resented his criticism. But it is

essential that you should realize that Clementi is not a crank or an unbalanced person. I specially selected him for Hong Kong in view of impending trouble on the double ground of his intimate and quite exceptional knowledge of the Chinese and of his general ability and judgment. It is quite possible that he may be wrong and incapable of seeing things from the broader point of view from which we can regard them here. But if he takes the line he does I am convinced it is not because of some personal defect of judgment or temper, but because that is how the situation is bound to strike anyone in the position of Governor of Hong Kong -- a position both of great responsibility and also of unique, if possibly limited, facilities for judging the situation. To put it bluntly, you or I or Austen would probably be taking the same view if we were in his position." Amery to Baldwin, 3 February 1927, F.O. 800/260 Chamberlain Papers, PRO Five months later he told Chamberlain that Clementi "is an able man and quite capable of correcting mistaken impressions." Amery to Chamberlain, 21 July 1927, F.O. 800/261 Chamberlain papers, PRO.

28. Quoted in Louis, pp. 131-32.

29. British estimations of the United States sank to a new low during the weeks surrounding the Hankow crisis. Lampson gave the following opinion to Chamberlain of an American proposal to get assurances from Chinese military leaders to respect the safety of foreign lives and property: "I trust you will have no delusion as to [the] futility of any such assurance from various Chinese military leaders. If for the sake of American opinion you feel it desirable to give [the] appearance of taking [the] State Department's suggestion seriously that is another matter. But so far as its intrinsic merits are concerned I must repeat my opinion that it is unpractical and typical [*sic*] American." Pratt minuted, "Sir M. Lampson takes exactly the same view as we do of the State Department's demarche." Lampson to Chamberlain, 4 February 1927, F.O. 371/12401, F 1101/2/10, PRO. One month before, Robert Vansittart had given an unflattering account of American policy makers: "Mr. Kellogg himself is what he was, only a little more so with age: amiable and irritable by turns, lacking in strength, something of an old woman "uncertain, coy and hard to please"--very hard sometimes. . . . The personnel of the State Department is--with much goodwill--incapable of changing these tendencies or of putting backbone into their chief. (It must always be remembered how staggeringly weak the Administration is in the United States). The material is not there not even such the stuff as dreams are made of. Mr. [Nelson T.] Johnson, the head of the Far Eastern

Department, I found very friendly and well disposed, but quite lacking in weight." Vansittart minute, 1 January 1927, F.O. 371/12398, F 39/2/10, PRO.

30. Chamberlain to Lampson, 24 March 1927, F.O. 371/12424, F 2460/36/10, PRO. G. Mounsey minuted, and Wellesley agreed that "there would be great outcry here in the event of a clash between our troops and *any* [emphasis in original] Chinese forces, if it could be shown that we had relaxed in any way rather than strengthened our vigilance. And it must be directed quite impartially."

31. MacMurray to Kellogg, 24 March 1927, 893.00 Nanking/3, FRUS 1927 vol. 2, pp. 146-48.

32. Quoted in Louis, p. 133.

33. Note marked "For Cabinet" initialed "A.C.," 5 May 1927, F.O. 371/12425, F 4762/36/10, PRO.

34. Lampson to Chamberlain, 25 December 1927, F.O. 371/12412, F 9418/2/10, PRO.

35. Mounsey minute under Lampson to Chamberlain, 25 December 1927, F.O. 371/12412, F 9418/2/10, PRO. Earlier in the year Lampson had written that "MacMurray, the American, is an extremely nice fellow, but has the disadvantage of being too much of an expert, and I think has been turned down by his own government so frequently -- indeed every time that he has tried to take any sort of initiative -- that his spirit is broken." Lampson to Chamberlain, 23 February 1927 F.O. 800, 260 Chamberlain Papers, P.R.O.

36. Gennaro Falconneri, "Reactions to Revolution: Japanese Attitudes and Foreign Policy Toward China 1924-1927" (Ph.D. diss., University of Michigan, 1967), pp. 308-10.

37. Ibid., p. 363.

38. Ibid., p. 311.

39. William F. Norton, "The Tanaka Cabinet's China Policy, 1927-1929" (Ph.D. diss., Columbia University, 1969), pp. 218, 223.

40. Iriye, *After Imperialism,* p. 209.

41. Norton, pp. 229-30.

42. See Tilley to Chamberlain, 21 and 26 January 1928, F.O. 405/256, F 335/20/10 and F 406/20 10, and Chamberlain to Tilley, 27 January 1928, F.O. 405/256, F 335/20/10, PRO. There was, however, some skepticism in the Foreign Office over Japan's motives: "This conference would appear to be in the nature of a stalking horse. The Japanese know quite well that unanimity is unobtainable and they will get all the kudos they can by calling it

while taking no blame for its failure." C. E. Steele minute under Tilley to Chamberlain, 31 January 1928, F.O. 371/13178, F 1124/20/10, PRO.

43. Kellogg to Mayer, 18 February 1928, 893.113/1072, FRUS 1928, vol. 2, p. 295.

44. Mayer to Kellogg, 23 February 1928, 893.113/1077, FRUS 1928, pp. 296-97. In the middle of March, W. R. Peck wrote a memorandum on the status of the embargo expressing the belief that "(1) the embargo has failed in its objectives; (2) that there is slight reason to suppose that it may be made successful, and (3) that its existence is detrimental to the United States." Peck went so far as to say that "viewed dispassionately, the events of the last nine years in China seem to indicate beyond doubt that no settlement of China's internal problems can be arrived at except through the issue, among the Chinese, of armed conflict." He concluded that the Division of Far Eastern Affairs believed that the United States "would be better off if the Agreement did not exist or if by any creditable process the United States might cease to be a party to it." 12 March 1928 Memorandum, 893.113/1101, DSNA.

45. For Germany's acceptance, see Schurman to Kellogg, 30 April 1928, 893.113/1117, DSNA. The Soviet Union denied that it had ever imported arms into China. MacVeagh reported that the Japanese vice minister for foreign affairs "did not appear to regard [the Soviet statement] with any degree of seriousness." MacVeagh to Kellogg, 11 April 1928, 893.113/1110, DSNA.

46. McCormack, pp. 214-15.

47. The Diplomatic Corps had met at the end of November to consider ending the embargo at the request of the French minister. See MacMurray to Kellogg, 23 November and 5 December 1928, 893.113/1155, DSNA, and Lampson to Chamberlain, 29 November 1928, F.O. 405/260, F 404/120/10, PRO.

48. See Toller minute and minutes, 2 January 1929, F.O. 371/13922, F 128/120/10, Lampson to Chamberlain, 4 January 1929, F.O. 405/260, F 127/10/10, Chamberlain to Lampson, 19 January 1929, F.O. 405/260, F 128/120/10, PRO.

49. Lampson to Chamberlain, 8 February 1929, F.O. 405/260, F 699/120/10, PRO. The Japanese sought to postpone a decision arguing that the Nanking government was not yet effective. See Lampson to Chamberlain, 13 February 1929, F.O. 371/13922, F 1604/120/10, PRO.

50. Lampson to Chamberlain, 2 April 1929, F.O. 371/13922,

F 1592/120/10, PRO.   After the Japanese had unofficially informed the British that they would agree to cancel the embargo, W. Stark Toller minuted that "this is a very satisfactory development; it looks as though tomorrow may see the funeral." See the minutes under Tilley to Chamberlain, 18 April 1929, F.O. 405/261, F 1919/120/10, PRO.   See also Lampson to Chamberlain, 19 April 1929, F.O. 405/261, F 1927/120/10, PRO.

10

Conclusion

Was the China arms embargo a failure or success for the United States? In answering this question, scholars, as well as contemporary observers, jumped to the conclusion that the policy failed because weapons entered China throughout the decade of the embargo's existence. But this negative assessment ignores the fact that the embargo had accomplished one of its goals long before evasion of the agreement became more prevalent in the 1920s. Before criticizing the embargo, one must take into account the state of affairs in China that necessitated the policy in the first place.

In the years before World War I, China was one of the many battlegrounds over which the powers contested the "great game of empire." While the competition for concessions and contracts was ruthless, it remained largely peaceful. For the powers, at least the semblance of cooperation had to be maintained; few could forget the horrors of the Boxer Rebellion, which underscored the precarious position of foreigners living in China. In order to preserve their position in the country, the powers sought to maintain a unified diplomatic front vis-à-vis the Chinese. At the same time they regulated their own conduct to prevent an imbalance in the status quo that could lead to a fratricidal strife dangerous to all foreigners.

With the overthrow of the Manchu dynasty, however, it was increasingly difficult to maintain an equilibrium in China. The disintegration of Peking's authority and the rise of regional warlords presented the powers with the possibility of supporting particular factions in exchange for political or economic favors. World War I further undermined the status quo by removing all of the major European powers from active participation in Chinese affairs. Tokyo exploited this golden opportunity to the fullest, seeking to establish a paramount position in China while the other powers were distracted. In spite of Minister Reinsch's warnings to Washington of the threat to the Open Door policy, by the war's end the Japanese had not only more firmly entrenched themselves in Manchuria, but had also underwritten a sympathetic government in Peking.

The China arms embargo was born out of the efforts to roll back Japanese influence in China. The embargo, along with a ban on loans to China and the new Consortium, were designed to cut the pro-Japanese government of Tuan Ch'i-jui off from its source of weaponry and funding; once so isolated, it was only a matter of time before such an unpopular government fell from power. Thus Washington, with the support of London, designed the arms embargo primarily as a tool with which to force the Japanese to relinquish their ill-gotten wartime gains and to act once more as what Akira Iriye ironically termed a "respectable imperialist."[1]

Many Japanese, however, especially those in military circles, were reluctant to yield ground. Fortunately, Prime Minister Hara Takashi recognized the West's determination to restore the balance in China, and his government announced that Japan would cooperate. Had Hara not done so and had Japan continued to support Tuan openly while Western aid reached his opponents, China's civil war undoubtedly would have been much bloodier, and would have fostered a sharp deterioration in Japan's relations with the West; in this scenario, it is unlikely that attempts at international cooperation during the 1920s, such as the Washington Conference, would have been successful.

Power politics aside, humanitarian motives also played a role in the establishment of the embargo. Indeed the supporters of the embargo correctly feared that unless appropriate measures were taken, surplus war material from World War I would quickly find its way to China's battlefields. The West therefore hoped that an effective embargo would save Chinese lives and money, and force a peaceful settlement to the civil war.

The fall of Tuan's government in July of 1920, just fourteen months after the institution of the arms embargo, meant that the agreement had achieved its primary political goal for the United States. Nevertheless the powers could not simply terminate the agreement. On the one hand, China was as far as ever from reunification, which was the embargo's humanitarian goal; on the other hand, a prompt end to the embargo could only have embarrassed Tokyo, because it would have reinforced the perception that the agreement was solely an anti-Tuan, and hence anti-Japanese, policy. Thus the embargo remained in place, and as the civil war continued unabated, the agreement's shortcomings became ever more apparent.

The most fundamental flaw of the embargo stemmed from the fact that the original signatories were only the dozen powers with diplomatic representatives in Peking in May 1919. With a defeated Germany and an unrecognized Soviet Union not represented in China at that time, the embargo was an imperfect instrument from the very start. However, because those powers at Peking included the victors of World War I, who would for the moment dominate world affairs, their acceptance of the embargo sufficed to make the agreement initially effective and successful.

But as Europe returned to normal after the war, the temporary nature of the victorious great powers' ability to control the arms flow into China became apparent. Ultimately those powers that were apathetic or hostile to the agreement of 1919 sent arms to China in pursuit of lucrative profits and/or political gain.[2] Thus, as Secretary of State Kellogg indicated in February of 1928, "the great changes that have occurred in the international situation," mainly the ability of many more powers to export arms than in 1919, undermined the embargo's effectiveness.[3]

Nearly as damaging to the embargo as non-compliance was disagreement among the signatory powers over what exactly could not be shipped to China. The ambiguous phrase "arms and munitions of war" was the starting point for controversies over disparate items ranging from aircraft to arsenal equipment. In the end such bickering served only to encourage the embargo's detractors while embarrassing and distracting its defenders.

The embargo's supporters also had to defend the agreement against attacks from businessmen in their own countries. From a commercial perspective, the embargo did penalize manufacturers and shippers in countries enforcing the embargo and benefitted rivals in non-observing countries. On the whole, however, material arguments did not dissuade those who supported the embargo as the morally and politically proper policy to pursue.

Criticism of the embargo for working to the advantage of the bolsheviks, however, was much more difficult to answer. By 1925 the spread of Soviet influence into China, accompanied by lavish arms shipments, was a serious concern. The agreement's opponents charged, with some justification, that the embargo, which had originally helped to end Japanese predominance in China, now promoted the spread of bolshevism by preventing Western aid from reaching anti-communist Chinese.

While deploring Soviet arms shipments, both Washington and London nevertheless decided to maintain the embargo. Resisting the temptation to take action and intervene in the conflict, the embargo's defenders argued that to raise the prohibition in favor of anti-communist factions would do more harm than good; undoubtedly recalling the anti-Japanese sentiments aroused in China by Tokyo's aid to Tuan, Washington and London decided to hope for the best by retaining the embargo and maintaining an impartial stance. Although Washington apparently wavered in its support for the embargo when confronted with Chiang Kai-shek's Northern Expedition in the summer of 1926, in the end the United States shied away from assuming the responsibility for terminating the agreement. Ultimately, the decision not to abandon the embargo paid handsome dividends when Chiang expelled the communists from the Kuomintang in the spring of 1927. As Chiang expanded his control in China, Washington showed even less interest in the embargo. When London, after having recognized Chiang's government, finally decided to initiate the termination of the agreement, Washington and the powers agreed to lift the embargo in spite of Japanese resistance.

For the United States, then, what had the China arms embargo accomplished and at what cost? Under Chiang Kai-shek, the Chinese had established a government dominated neither by the Japanese nor Soviets, and arguably friendly to the United States. Such political success far outweighed the material losses American commercial interests had suffered because of embargo restrictions. Although in the long run Chiang would not provide China with the kind of leadership Washington had hoped for, this could not have been foreseen during the 1920s. Rather, from Washington's perspective, the advent of Chiang seemed to portend the end of China's long civil war on terms favorable to the United States. Thus one can argue that the embargo served as an effective tool of American foreign policy.

A much more difficult question to answer is whether or not the embargo benefited the Chinese. Would the civil war have ended sooner if the warlords had enjoyed unlimited access to arms markets? Would Chiang or a more effective leader have come to power with less bloodshed and dislocation? No answer to these or similar questions can be conclusive. Yet one can speculate that it is unlikely that the conflict would have been any shorter had more weaponry entered China, and the number of casualties would have increased greatly. Thus one can consider the embargo to have succeeded both as a humanitarian measure and as a means to further the interests of the United States.

NOTES

1. Iriye, *After Imperialism*, p. 9.

2. One cannot entirely blame the Diplomatic Corps at Peking for having constructed an imperfect instrument, because some countries that exported arms to China in the 1920s, such as Czechoslovakia, did not even exist when the arms embargo was formulated in May 1919. Furthermore those attempting to evade the embargo were quick to spot loopholes in the agreement; W. Stark Toller minuted in June 1928 that "the arms traffickers appear to have discovered another unstopped hole in the Free City of Danzig, which has never been invited to accede in the Arms Embargo Agreement." Toller minute under Lindley to Chamberlain, 19 June 1928, F.O. 371/13180, F 3297/20/10, PRO.

3. Kellogg to Mayer, 18 February 1928, 893.113/1072, FRUS 1928, vol. 2, pp. 294-95.

Bibliography

I. Manuscripts

British Museum, London, England
        Arthur J. Balfour papers

Cornell University, Ithaca, New York
        Jacob Gould Schurman papers

Library of Congress, Washington, D.C.
        Bainbridge Colby papers
        Charles Evans Hughes papers
        Nelson T. Johnson papers
        Frank B. Kellogg papers
        Robert Lansing papers
        Breckenridge Long papers
        John Van Antwerp MacMurray papers

Public Record Office, Kew Gardens, England

        Sir Beilby Alston papers
        Sir Austen Chamberlain papers
        Marquess Curzon of Kedleston papers
        Sir Charles Eliot papers
        Sir John Jordan papers
        Sir Walter Langley papers
        James Ramsay MacDonald papers

II. Published Documents

Conference on the Limitation of Armament, Washington, November 12, 1921 -- February 6, 1922. Washington: Government Printing Office, 1922.

Papers Relating to the Foreign Relations of the United States, 1916-1929. Washington: Government Printing Office.

Link, Arthur S. et al., eds. *The Papers of Woodrow Wilson*. Princeton, N.J.: Princeton University Press, 1966-1989.

MacMurray, John Van Antwerp, ed. *Treaties and Agreements with and Concerning China, 1894-1919*. 2 vols. New York: Oxford University Press, 1921.

Woodward, E. L. & Rohan, Butler, eds. *Documents on British Foreign Policy, 1919-1939*. London: His Majesty's Stationary Office, 1956.

III. Books

Adler, Selig. *The Uncertain Giant 1921-1941; American Foreign Policy Between the Wars*. New York: MacMillan, 1965.

Atwater, Elton. *American Regulation of Arms Exports*. Washington, D.C.: Carnegie Endowment for International Peace, 1941.

Bamba, Nobuya. *Japanese Diplomacy in a Dilemma: New Light on Japan's China Policy, 1924-1929*. Vancouver: University of British Columbia Press, 1972.

Beers, Burton. *Vain Endeavor: Robert Lansing's Attempts to End the American-Japanese Rivalry*. Durham, N.C.: Duke University Press, 1962.

Borg, Dorothy. *American Policy and the Chinese Revolution, 1925-1928*. New York: Macmillan, 1947. 2nd ed. 1968.

Botjer, George. *A Short History of Nationalist China, 1919-49*. New York: G. P. Putnam's Sons, 1979.

Brandes, Joseph. *Herbert Hoover and Economic Diplomacy; Department of Commerce Policy, 1921-1928*. Pittsburgh, Penn.: University of Pittsburgh Press, 1962.

Briscoe, Jerry. *Economic Interests in British Relations with China, 1921-1928*. Chicago: University of Chicago Press, 1954.

Buhite, Russell. *Nelson T. Johnson and American Policy Toward China, 1925-1941*. East Lansing: Michigan State University Press, 1968.

Burns, Richard, and Edward Bennett, eds. *Diplomats in Crisis: United States-Chinese-Japanese Relations, 1919-1941*. Santa Barbara, Calif.: ABC-Clio, 1976.

Cameron, Meribeth, et al., eds. *China, Japan and the Powers*. New York: Ronald Press, 1952, 2nd ed. 1960.

Campbell, Charles S., Jr. *Special Business Interests and the Open Door Policy*. New Haven, Conn.: Yale University Press, 1951.

Chan, Anthony. *Arming the Chinese: The Western Armaments Trade in Warlord China, 1920-1928*. Vancouver: University of British Columbia Press, 1982.

_____. "Chinese Warlords and the Western Armaments Trade in Warlord China, 1920-1928." Ph.D. dissertation, York University (Canada), 1980.

Chi, Hsi-Sheng. *Warlord Politics in China, 1916-1928*. Stanford, Calif.: Stanford University Press, 1976.

Chi, Madeleine. *China Diplomacy, 1914-1918*. Cambridge: East Asian Research Center, Harvard University, distributed by Harvard University Press, 1970.

Cohen, Warren. *America's Response to China; An Interpretive History of Sino-American Relations*. New York: Wiley, 1971.

Conant, Charles. *The United States and the Orient; The Nature of the Economic Problem*. Port Washington: Kennikat, 1971 reprint of 1900 edition.

Coox, Alvin, and Hilary Conroy, eds. *China and Japan: Search for Balance Since World War I*. Santa Barbara, Calif.: ABC-Clio, 1978.

Costigliola, Frank. *Awkward Dominion: American Political, Economic, and Cultural Relations with Europe, 1919-1939*. Ithaca, N.Y.: Cornell University Press, 1984.

Cronon, E. David, ed. *The Cabinet Diaries of Josephus Daniels, 1913-1921*. Lincoln: University of Nebraska Press, 1963.

Crowley, James. *Japan's Quest for Autonomy; National Security and Foreign Policy 1930-1938*. Princeton, N.J.: Princeton University Press, 1966.

Curry, Roy Watson. *Woodrow Wilson and Far Eastern Policy, 1913-1921*. New York: Bookman Associates, 1957.

Dayer, Roberta. *Bankers and Diplomats in China, 1917-1925; The Anglo-American Relationship*. London: Frank Cass, 1981.

DeAngelis, Richard. "Jacob Gould Schurman and American Policy Toward China, 1921-1925." Ph.D. dissertation, St. John's University, 1975.

Dennett, Tyler. *Americans in Eastern Asia; A Critical Study of the Policy of the United States*. New York: Macmillan, 1922.

Dignan, Donald. *New Perspectives on British Far Eastern Policy, 1913-1919*. St. Lucia, Brisbane: University of Queensland Press, 1969.

Duroselle, Jean-Baptiste. *From Wilson to Roosevelt; Foreign Policy of the United States 1913-1945.* Nancy Oelker, trans. Cambridge: Harvard University   Press, 1963.

Ellis, Lewis Ethan. *Frank B. Kellogg and American Foreign Relations 1925-1929.* New Brunswick, N.J.: Rutgers University Press, 1961.

Fairbank, John King, ed. *The Cambridge History of China.* 19 vols. Cambridge: Cambridge University Press, 1986-87.

_____ . *The United States and China.* Cambridge: Harvard University Press, 4th ed., 1979.

Falconeri, Gennaro. "Reactions to Revolution: Japanese Attitudes and Foreign Policy Toward China 1924-1927." Ph.D. diss., University of Michigan, 1967.

Feis, Herbert. *Diplomacy of the Dollar: First Era, 1919-1932.* Baltimore, Md.: Johns Hopkins University Press, 1950.

Ferrell, Robert. *American Diplomacy in the Great Depression; Hoover-Stimson Foreign Policy, 1929-1933.* New Haven, Conn.: Yale University Press, 1957.

Foner, Eric. *Spanish-Cuban-American War and the Birth of American Imperialism, 1985-1902.* New York: Monthly Review Press, 1972.

Gage, Daniel James. "Paul S. Reinsch and Sino-American Relations." Ph.D. diss., Stanford University, 1939.

Gardner, Lloyd C. *Wilson and Revolutions, 1913-1921.* Philadelphia: J. B. Lippincott, 1976.

George, Brian Thomas. "The Open Door and the Rise of Chinese Nationalism, 1917-1928." Ph.D. dissertation, University of New Mexico, 1977.

Griswold, A. Whitney. *The Far Eastern Policy of the United States.* New Haven, Conn.: Yale University Press, 1938.

Hoff-Wilson, Joan. *American Business and Foreign Policy, 1920-33.* Lexington: Kentucky University Press, 1972.

Hogan, Michael. *Informal Entente: The Private Structure of Cooperation in Anglo-American Economic Diplomacy.* Columbia, Missouri: University of Missouri Press, 1977.

Hunt, Michael. *The Making of a Special Relationship: The United States and China to 1914.* New York: Columbia University Press, 1983.

Iriye, Akira, ed. *The Chinese and the Japanese. Essays in Political and Cultural Interactions.* Princeton, N.J.: Princeton University Press, 1980.

_____ . *After Imperialism: The Search for a New Order in the Far East, 1921-1931.* Cambridge, Mass.: Harvard University Press, 1965.

_____. *Across the Pacific: An Inner History of American-East Asian Relations.* New York: Harcourt, Brace and World, 1967.

Jansen, Marius. *Japan and its World: Two Centuries of Change.* Princeton, N.J.: Princeton University Press, 1980.

_____. *The Japanese and Sun Yat-sen.* Cambridge: Harvard University Press, 1954.

LaFeber, Walter. *The New Empire: An Interpretation of American Expansion, 1860-1898.* Ithaca, N.Y.: Cornell University Press, 1963.

Lansing, Robert. *The War Memoirs of Robert Lansing Secretary of State.* New York: Bobbs-Merrill, 1935.

Link, Arthur S., ed. *Woodrow Wilson and a Revolutionary World, 1913-1921.* Chapel Hill: University of North Carolina Press, 1982.

Lippmann, Walter. *United States Foreign Policy: Shield of the Republic.* Boston: Little, Brown, & Co., 1943.

Louis, William Roger. *British Strategy in the Far East, 1919-1939.* Oxford: Clarendon Press, 1971.

Lowe, Peter. *Britain in the Far East: A Survey from 1819 to the Present.* London: Longman, 1981.

_____. *Great Britain and Japan, 1911-1915: A Study of British Far Eastern Policy.* New York: St. Martin's Press, 1969.

Mahan, Alfred Thayer. *The Problem of Asia and its Effect on International Policies.* London: Sampson Low, Marsten & Co, 1900.

May, Ernest R., and James C. Thomson, Jr., eds., *American-East Asian Relations: A Survey.* Cambridge: Harvard University Press, 1972.

McCormack, Gavan. *Chang Tso-lin in Northeast China 1911-1928: China, Japan and the Manchuria Idea.* Stanford, Calif.: Stanford University Press, 1977.

McCormick, Thomas. *China Market: America's Quest for Informal Empire, 1893-1901.* Chicago: Quadrangle Books, 1967.

Norton, William F. "The Tanaka Cabinet's China Policy, 1927-1929." Ph.D. diss., Columbia University, 1969.

Perkins, Dexter. *America and Two Wars.* Boston: Little, Brown, & Co., 1944.

Pugach, Noel H. *Paul S. Reinsch; Open Door Diplomat in Action.* Millwood: KTO Press, 1979.

Pusey, Merlo. *Charles Evans Hughes.* 2 vols. New York: Macmillan, 1951.

Pye, Lucian. *Warlord Politics: Conflict and Coalition in the Modernization of Republican China.* New York: Praeger Publishers, 1971.

Reinsch, Paul S. *An American Diplomat in China.* Garden City, N.Y.:
    Doubleday, 1922.
Remer, Charles. *Foreign Investments in China.* New York: Macmillan,
    1933.
Scanlan, Patrick John. "No Longer a Treaty Port: Paul S. Reinsch and
    China, 1913-1919." Ph.D. dissertation, University of Wisconsin,
    1973.
Sheridan, James. *Chinese Warlord: The Career of Feng Yu-hsiang.*
    Stanford, Calif.: Stanford University Press, 1966.
_____. *China in Disintegration: The Republican Era in Chinese History,*
    1912-1949. New York: Free Press, 1975.
Smith, Daniel M. *Aftermath of War: Bainbridge Colby and Wilsonian*
    Diplomacy, 1920-1921. Philadelphia: American Philosophical
    Society, 1970.
Stremski, Richard. "Britain's China Policy, 1920-1928." Ph.D. diss.,
    University of Wisconsin, Madison 1968.
Takeshi, Matsuda. "Woodrow Wilson's Dollar Diplomacy in the Far
    East: The New Chinese Consortium, 1917-1921." Ph.D.
    dissertation, University of Wisconsin (Madison), 1979.
Varg, Paul. *The Closing of the Door: Sino-American Relations 1936-*
    1946. East Lansing: Michigan State University Press, 1973.
_____. *The Making of a Myth: The United States China, 1897-1912.*
    East Lansing: Michigan State University Press, 1968.
Whiting, Allen. *Soviet Policies in China 1917-1924.* New York:
    Columbia University Press, 1954.
Williams, William Appleman. *The Tragedy of American Diplomacy.* 2d
    ed., New York: Dell, 1972.
Young, Ernest P. *The Presidency of Yuan Shih-K'ai: Liberalism and*
    Dictatorship in early Republican China. Ann Arbor: University
    of Michigan Press, 1977.
Young, John Williams. "The Japanese Military and the China Policy of
    the Hara Cabinet, 1918-1921." Ph.D. dissertation, University of
    Washington, 1971.

IV. Articles

Altman, Albert, and Harold Schiffrin. "Sun Yat-sen and the Japanese:
    1914-1916." *Modern Asian Studies* 6 (1972) : 385-400.
Bix, Herbert. "Japanese Imperialism and the Manchurian Economy,
    1900-1931." *The China Quarterly* 51 (1972): 425-43.
Chi, Madeleine. "Bureaucratic Capitalists in Operation: Ts'au Ju-lin
    and his New Communications Clique, 1916-1919." *Journal of*
    Asian Studies 34 (1975): 675-88.

Coble, Parks. "Chiang Kai-shek and the Anti-Japanese Movement in China: Zou Tau-fen and the National Salvation Association, 1931-1937." *Journal of Asian Studies* 44 (1985): 293-310.

Davis, Clarence. "Financing Imperialism: British and American Bankers as Vectors of Imperial Expansion in China, 1908-1920." *Business History Review* 55 (1982): 236-64.

_____. "Limits of Effacement: Britain and the Problem of American Cooperation and Competition in China, 1915-1917." *Pacific Historical Review*. 48 (1979): 47-64.

Dayer, Roberta. "The British War Debts to the United States and the Anglo-Japanese Alliance, 1920-1923." *Pacific Historical Review* 45 (1976): 569-95.

Field, James. "American Imperialism: The Worst Chapter in Almost Any Book." *American Historical Review* 83 (1978): 644-83.

George, Brian. "The State Department and Sun Yat-sen: American Policy and the Revolutionary Disintegration of China, 1920-1924." *Pacific Historical Review* 46 (1977): 387-408.

McCormick, Thomas. "Insular Imperialism and the Open Door: The China Market and the Spanish-American War." *Pacific Historical Review* 32 (1963): 155-69.

Metallo, Michael. "American Missionaries, Sun Yat-sen, and the Chinese Revolution." *Pacific Historical Review* 47 (1978): 261-82.

Ninkovich, Frank. "Ideology, the Open Door and Foreign Policy." *Diplomatic History* 6 (1982): 185-208.

Pugach, Noel. "Anglo-American Aircraft Competition and the China Arms Embargo, 1919-1921." *Diplomatic History* 2 (1978): 351-71.

_____. "Making the Open Door Work: Paul S. Reinsch in China, 1913-1919." *Pacific Historical Review* 38 (1969): 157-75.

Stremski, Richard. "Britain and Warlordism in China: Relations with Feng Yu-hsiang, 1921-1928." *Journal of Oriental Studies* 11 (1973): 91-106.

Treadgold, Donald. "The United States and East Asia: A Theme with Variations." *Pacific Historical Review* 49 (1980): 1-28.

Varg, Paul. "Sino-American Relations Past and Present." *Diplomatic History* 4 (1980): 101-12.

Williams, William Appleman. "China and Japan: A Challenge and a Choice of the Nineteen Twenties." *Pacific Historical Review* 26 (1957): 259-79.

Index

About the Author

STEPHEN J. VALONE is Assistant Professor of History at St. John Fisher College in Rochester, New York. Specializing in United States diplomatic history, Dr. Valone has written several articles in his field of interest.